# What Was in Buddha's Left Hand?

Tantric teachings to transform
neurosis into sanity

# What people are saying about

# What Was in Buddha's Left Hand?

*What Was in Buddha's Left Hand?* builds on Ira Rechtshaffer's many years as a psychotherapist and is a fruitful doorway to bring the elements from Tibetan Buddhist psychology into modern understanding.
**Jack Kornfield**

It gives me great pleasure to endorse this book on the vast vision and minute particulars of the mandala principle. This important and comprehensive work illuminates the many aspects— psychological, elemental and sensory—of the five wisdom energies. We are indebted to Ira Rechtshaffer for contributing to our understanding of these profound teachings to bring about an embodied wholeness as well as a cosmic understanding.
**Irini Rockwell,** author of *The Five Wisdom Energies: A Buddhist Way of Understanding Personalities, Emotions, and Relationships* and *Natural Brilliance: A Buddhist System for Uncovering Your Strengths and Letting Them Shine*

I love and deeply respect *What Was in Buddha's Left Hand?* This is an exquisitely wise and down-to-earth book that unifies heart and mind, body and spirit. [Dr. Rechtshaffer demonstrates] that all experiences in life, the 10,000 joys and sorrows, are the greatest of teachers. This book is not about spiritually or psychologically bypassing life; instead it offers us guidance for how to embrace it all to discover the awakened heart (Buddha) within.
**Bob Stahl, PhD,** co-author of *A Mindfulness-Based Stress Reduction Workbook, Living With Your Heart Wide Open, Calming the Rush of Panic, A Mindfulness-Based Stress Reduction Workbook for Anxiety,* and *MBSR Every Day*

In *What Was in Buddha's Left Hand?* Dr. Rechtshaffer brings together four decades of Buddhist study and practice, alongside depth psychological and clinical experience, to share these timeless teachings in a way that is enjoyable, vivid, practical, and accessible to the Western psyche. Readers new to Buddhism and other spiritual traditions, as well as seasoned practitioners, will find nuggets of insight and relevant perspectives from this timeless tradition as conveyed through contemporary and everyday examples.

**Mariana Caplan, PhD, MFT,** author of *Yoga & Psyche: Integrating the Paths of Yoga and Psychology for Healing, Transformation, and Joy* and *Eyes Wide Open: Cultivating Discernment on the Spiritual Path*

Dr. Ira Rechtshaffer offers us a deep, personal, and illuminating exploration of the Five Wisdoms as they arise at the heart of all human experience. His presentation is fresh and engaging, with methods to incorporate these dimensions of experience in helpful ways in our complex human lives. I recommend this book for all who are interested in more in-depth understanding of Buddhism and its application to life, but also for those engaged in inner exploration from other traditions.

**James Sacamano, MD,** author of *Getting Back to Wholeness, The Treasure of Inner Health* and *The Power of a Meaningful Life,* and teachings on Medicine Buddha at medicinebuddhatoday.com

## Also by Ira Rechtshaffer:

Mindfulness and Madness: Money, Food, Sex, and the Sacred Changemakers ISBN 978-1-78535-086-3

# What Was in Buddha's Left Hand?

Tantric teachings to transform
neurosis into sanity

Ira Rechtshaffer

CHANGEMAKERS
BOOKS

Winchester, UK
Washington, USA

JOHN HUNT PUBLISHING

First published by Changemakers Books, 2020
Changemakers Books is an imprint of John Hunt Publishing Ltd., No. 3 East Street,
Alresford, Hampshire SO24 9EE, UK
office@jhpbooks.com
www.johnhuntpublishing.com
www.changemakers-books.com

For distributor details and how to order please visit the 'Ordering' section on our website.

Text copyright: Ira Rechtshaffer 2018

ISBN: 978 1 78904 311 2
978 1 78904 312 9 (ebook)
Library of Congress Control Number: 2018964354

A CIP catalogue record for this book is available from the British Library.

Design: Stuart Davies

UK: Printed and bound by CPI Group (UK) Ltd, Croydon, CR0 4YY
US: Printed and bound by Thomson-Shore, 7300 West Joy Road, Dexter, MI 48130

We operate a distinctive and ethical publishing philosophy in
all areas of our business, from our global network of authors to
production and worldwide distribution.

# Contents

This book is dedicated to Chogyam Trungpa Rinpoche, who transmitted the teachings of the five buddha families or wisdom energies to Westerners, opening our eyes to their power to transform confusion into wisdom, and to the teachers of the Tantric Buddhist tradition who continue to transplant the Buddhist teachings of liberation in the West.

# Acknowledgments

I am grateful to Nancy Carleton, my faithful and highly accomplished editor, who has been tireless in her efforts to support and encourage me through this process. To Laura Duggan, who has provided helpful editorial suggestions and constructive criticism, and to my dear friends, Margot Iseman and Cynthia Barbaccia, who took the time to carefully read my manuscript, offering support and necessary corrections.

# Preface

As a young man I secretly yearned for some way or method—some special key—that would permit me to develop myself throughout the remainder of my life, whether in times of scarcity or abundance, illness or health, or when nothing else seemed to work to help make sense of my life. I imagined myself stranded on an isolated island, and wondered whether there was a discipline or a way of being that could enable me to make creative use of my time, to cultivate the deepest aspects of myself, so that I could evolve my spiritual path until my last breath.

Many years ago, in the mid-1970s, Chogyam Trungpa Rinpoche, a Tibetan Buddhist tantric master, taught a cycle of teachings known as the five elements or five wisdom energies, which spoke directly to the quest I'd been on for many years. This book is about this particular body of teachings from the Buddhist tantric tradition, which enables us to be more of who we are under any circumstances. It describes and explains the process of awakening to the wonder and beauty of the experience we're already having in this very moment.

Although the five elements within us—space, water, earth, fire, and wind—are expressions of wisdom energy and hold great gifts, we tend to develop a neurotic or distorted relationship with them. The five-element teachings offer a map for how to transform neurotic states of mind into their naturally elegant and exalted expressions. This is the left-hand path of Buddha.

The five elements function like a Rosetta stone, helping us decipher innumerable layers, aspects, and dimensions of ourselves. They reveal our psychospiritual anatomy so that we can tap our power centers and passionately express ourselves through everything that exists in our life, through our intimate relationships, our friendships, our livelihood, and through our personal projects and ambitions. At the same time, they teach

1

us how to suffer wisely during times of loneliness, loss, grief, confusion, and even illness. As we begin to tune into them, they unleash their power to animate and enliven our connection with our everyday life. Their living energy helps us to transform otherwise mundane events into occasions of appreciation. They inspire us to see, hear, and feel the world with refreshing openness so that we can step beyond our neurotic patterns.

My hope is that through this book and its contemplative exercises, you will experience how your five internal elements can be used in your everyday life to discover the forgotten wisdom and beauty inherent in ordinary experience. This path can inspire you to establish a more intimate relationship both with yourself and with your immediate environment. May these teachings help you, too, find the special key that enables you to develop yourself until your last breath.

# Introduction

In esoteric schools of practice, Buddha's right hand symbolizes the traditional and more widely accepted principles and practices of his teachings, or *dharma*, while the left-hand path refers to the more radical understanding and methods for discovering enlightenment where we'd least expect to find it. This left-hand body of methods, sometimes known as *tantra*, includes the teaching of the five elements—space, water, earth, fire, and wind—which give us practical methods for how to work skillfully with our neurotic patterns so that we can use their raw energy to fuel our spiritual journey and experience a more abundant life.

## The Five Wisdom Energies

The five elements are wisdom energies—that is, they are five expressions of the naturally sane or awakened aspects of ourselves. They aren't five different things but five interdependent aspects of one fundamental energy, the energy of life itself. At the same time, they are five fundamentally different ways of relating with experience, such as intuition (space element), unbiased perception (water element), sensation and feeling (earth element), desire or passion (fire element), and kinetic movement (wind element).

The five elements are also differing forms of intelligence that we all possess beyond IQ, such as spiritual intelligence (space), linguistic or analytic intelligence (water), somatic or sensory intelligence (earth), interpersonal or social intelligence (fire), and kinesthetic intelligence (wind).

With the exception of the space element, each of the elements has both masculine and feminine aspects, which help balance their complementary aspects. The more we're able to integrate both the masculine and feminine energies, the less neurotic

3

suffering and anguish we experience, the more holistic our vision of life, and the greater our capacity for creativity.

Further, the elements are embodied in five differing emotional patterns, five relational strategies, five fundamental cognitive distortions, and five basic motivations that shape our behavior. In this book, we'll be exploring these aspects of the elements with the goal of enabling you to know yourself better and ultimately use the formerly rejected aspects of your personality as part of your path of spiritual awakening, thus allowing you to live a life of greater integrity and wholeness.

One of the historical problems in numerous spiritual traditions has been that the enlightenment experience doesn't necessarily liberate the awakened individual from the shadow aspects of personality, nor from the collective conditioning of culture. In other words, the realization of the enlightenment isn't always symmetrical and doesn't always illuminate the entirety of the awakened human being.

There have been numerous cases both historical and contemporary where the depth dimension of mind outshone the latent neuroses and limiting cultural biases of awakened individuals, as long as they remained centered in their depth. Yet, their relationship to sex and intimacy, food and substance, money and power, remained at an earlier developmental level, as demonstrated by behaviors that were less than enlightened.

Waking up to our most profound spiritual potential needs to be fully embodied so that the awakened energy can infiltrate the shadowy corners of personality to transform all within us that's developmentally junior to the enlightened mind. Further, the light of wisdom needs to illuminate the pernicious blind spots embedded within our culture, such as patriarchal bias, sexism, racism, abuses of power, and the devaluation of the nonhuman world within the ecological web. The radical methods of the left-hand path, including embodying the five wisdom energies, are supremely effective tools to smoke out the hidden pockets of both ourselves and our culture so that they can meet with the light of awareness.

## Buddhist Psychology

Although all of us have space, water, earth, fire, and wind dimensions within our personality, according to Buddhist psychology we come into this life with a particular sensitivity to one of the elements and embody its characteristics in both its neurotic and exalted aspects. In this regard, we could say that some of us are space personalities, while others are water, earth, fire, or wind types. In other words, one of the elements is usually dominant by virtue of our genetic inheritance, early conditioning, and unique soulful design. Because most of us have disconnected from our essential or awakened nature early in life, each personality style is a metaphor, as we try to compensate for abandoning our own Buddha nature—the part of us that is already liberated—by trying to replicate its qualities.

I think it's more accurate to regard the qualities of each of the five elements as applying to *all of us* in varying degrees, so that we can recognize and understand the patterns driving us to destinations not of our conscious choice. There are circumstances, relationships, and periods of our life when a particular element's qualities are dominant in our experience. As you read the book and begin to become acquainted with the elements and their energies, you may find that one of them clearly stands out for you, and yet you will likely relate to some of the material for each of the five elements.

In Buddhist tradition it's said that neurosis and wisdom, *samsara* (the Sanskrit term for collective neurosis) and *nirvana* (the state of liberation from neurosis, or sanity), originate from the same source. Consequently, if we understand the complexities of our personality, the quality of our interpersonal relationships, and the meaning behind our behaviors, then nirvana becomes redundant. Nirvana is nothing other than samsara *fully* revealed.

This realization is one of the secrets of the left-hand approach—how to be a complete human being capable of holding the tension between the good and bad, the ugly and the beautiful, our creative and destructive aspects, as well as the conscious and nonconscious domains within ourselves.

There's an alternative to the madness of samsara. The left-hand path asks us to disrobe in full view of the raw and rugged reality of life, and the teaching of the five elements provides us with the means to do this. As we dare to drop our defenses we become receptive to what's before us so that we can more accurately reflect *what is*. The recipe for how to do this was handed down to us several millennia ago by Buddha, who recommended that we meet the world's nakedness with our own. The following brief review of Buddhist history and the emergence of the left-hand path will help you place the teachings of the five elements into their broader context.

## The Three Turnings of Buddha's Teachings

Many of the great Buddhist teachers have said that samsara is notorious for being without end. By reviewing the evolution of Buddha's teachings through its three developmental periods we can see how the subtleties of samsara or subtle neuroses are progressively overcome. Reviewing these three periods of Buddhism helps us transplant these precious teachings in our Western soil in the light of contemporary psychology. We're in a position to draw out the further implications of these ancient teachings that have remained implicit.

In the Vajrayana Buddhist tradition—the tradition of esoteric Buddhism associated with tantra—the teachings have been grouped into three major categories, known as the "three turnings" of the dharma wheel. In each successive turning of the wheel Buddha, or the Awakened One, emphasized an overarching theme, drawing out the more profound implications of his prior body of teachings. The later teachings made explicit what was only implicit in their earlier expression, and so there was no real contradiction between one turning and the next.

In the first turning Buddha introduced the foundational teachings of the *four noble truths*, which described and explained the truth of suffering but emphasized the path leading out of suffering. This path of renunciation encouraged practitioners to learn what to let go of and what to embrace, which cultivated a strong ethical sensibility. These teachings appeared to create a basic split between the suffering of ordinary life, or *samsara*, and the state of release from suffering, or *nirvana*. Meditation, contemplation, and right action guided practitioners across the turbulent ocean of samsara to the far shore of nirvana, implying that samsara and nirvana were opposites, although Buddha never stated this.

In the second turning, Buddha introduced the radical notion of *emptiness*, emphasizing that there was no real separation between samsara and nirvana. Truth or reality had no opposites, but was a seamless whole. Everyday life, with all of its desires, struggles, and conflicts, was no different from the enlightened state of nirvana when viewed with meditative awareness. This second turning offered a deeper, more penetrating understanding of the relationship between suffering and its release, between the individual personality and the doctrine of selflessness.

Because of the profound insight into the inseparability of self and other, the second-turning teachings emphasized not only emptiness but the need to extend compassion unconditionally to help all beings wake up spiritually. This was the *bodhisattva* ideal. Nevertheless, the second-turning teachings seemed to confer a transcendental quality to nirvana that privileged this exalted state while tending to devalue the bread-and-butter world of everyday life. The mysterious, unfathomable quality of emptiness could be used as a philosophical padding to protect practitioners from the raw-and-ragged edges of samsara, the conventional world.

The second turning viewed the world as having no underlying substance or reality, making it seemingly disappear within the immeasurable depth and vastness of emptiness. This perspective led the way to the third turning of the wheel, a series of teachings that offered an even more profound expression of the inseparability of suffering and liberation, neurosis and enlightenment. This more profound understanding of emptiness now invited back the nitty-gritty world to be fully appreciated, with all of its brilliant colors, textures, tastes, and aromas, as well as its conflicts and turbulent emotions.

The third turning proclaimed that wherever we find ourselves, no matter what the circumstances, we don't have to make strenuous efforts to escape the apparent limitations of worldly experience. Nirvana is found in the living energy of life, on the street level of worldly desires, conflicts, and turbulent emotions. A luminous energy sparkles through everyday experience to reveal that there's no corner of life that doesn't radiate Buddha essence. This truth formed the basis of the left-hand path, which appeared in some ways to contradict Buddha's fundamental teachings. Historically many of these methods went against the cultural, philosophical, and religious traditions of ancient India, and were subsequently outlawed as not being part of Buddha's teachings.

This third-turning teaching is radical in its implications. The very things that cause suffering and limitation—the very things that we've been trying to escape—we now understand to be the source of our freedom. The third turning helped practitioners to cultivate an attitude of sacredness with respect to the ingredients of ordinary life. It implied that they could indulge in the phenomenal world of the senses, in sexual activity and sensual pleasure, in order to reveal enlightened nature—the *suchness*, or *tathata* in Sanskrit—in the stuff of everyday life.

This left-hand spiritual path of tantra is dangerous because we could either suddenly awaken spiritually in the midst of the most mundane activities, or succumb to addictive indulgence in sensory pleasure. At worst, we could develop spiritual narcissism, justifying and rationalizing any manner of dysfunctional behavior, where everything is okay. Therefore, an essential point, especially for our contemporary time, is the necessity of incorporating the teachings of the first and second turnings on our path, so that we integrate discipline, higher ethics, compassion, and wisdom as we appreciate the world of the senses.

## The Buddhist Mandala and the Elements

The five wisdom energies, or elements, of the Buddhist *mandala* — a circular design that embodies our psychospiritual totality — provide a system of personal transformation that guides us in transmuting our distorted aspects into their naturally elegant expressions, a key quality of the left-hand path. These teachings give character and substance to the individual human person while simultaneously affording us a way to work with our neurotic patterns so that they may dawn as wisdom. They invite us to explore the world of the senses so central to the left-hand path.

Mandalas express the experience of intimate relationship among and between our many parts as well as our connection with our surroundings and our culture. In terms of a human being's design, we are the center of our experiential world, which is the space element. Whatever is in front of, behind, to the left of, and to the right of ourselves is represented by the four elements of water, fire, earth, and wind and the four cardinal directions.

The five elements act as living energies that animate the tangible forms of the outer world as well as our inner world of thoughts and feelings. The good news is that this teaching isn't just a theory, but something that you can experience right now in the privacy of your own home. You'll find the material in this book more meaningful and applicable to your daily life if you begin a regular meditation practice — if you don't already have one. Meditation practice can be quite ordinary and simple, and easy to integrate into your everyday life.

Meditation is a natural activity that's been practiced for thousands of years by people in diverse spiritual traditions. Meditation is the process of bringing your full attention to what you rarely give a moment's thought to—the experience you're having right now. The basic instruction is to find a quiet place in your home where there's little to distract you. Take a comfortably seated posture, with your eyes either open or closed, as you practice bringing your attention to what's happening moment by moment. Set the intention that you will sit in silence and stillness for ten to fifteen minutes, or longer if you feel motivated. Notice when you're thinking, or having a hunger pang in your stomach, or hearing the distant hum of traffic, or going over your agenda in your mind. When you notice that you're thinking or picking up on environmental stimuli, immediately let go of the thought, feeling, or sensation. Once you let go, continue exercising alertness and relaxation. To help you remain centered in the present, you can use the natural movement of your breath as a reminder to stay focused on the here and now.

I invite you to dive into the direct experience of this material through the following meditation, which evokes the energies of each of the five elements you'll be working with throughout the book. We are embodiments of Mother Nature, composed of her elements of space, water, earth, fire, and wind. These five basic energies manifest externally in the natural world and internally within our emotional, psychological, and spiritual dimensions. Becoming increasingly sensitive to the unique qualities of each of the elements, and attuning ourselves with its energy, we awaken our power centers to restore balance and wholeness to our life. The more these inner energies are brought into balance, the more we experience the natural world as sacred, ending the secret wish to escape from our life as it is. Let's get started!

## Meditation: The Five Elements in Action

Take a comfortably seated position, and allow yourself ten to fifteen minutes to sit in silence and stillness. Put your to-do list or daily agenda on hold for the duration of this time.

**Space:** Your life can unfold moment by moment only because there's a clearing in time and space, an open and formless dimension that accommodates you. This obvious but subtle truth of the space element expresses itself as a sense of openness and presence, the freedom of not having to know anything or figure anything out. It's the ground zero of meditation practice.

It manifests in the midst of your everyday activities, when you suddenly become aware of a gap—a pause in the usual momentum that drives you. There need not be any form or shape to this experience as a moment of silence and stillness punctuates your usual busyness. Taken by surprise you could find yourself enjoying the open potential of the unfolding moment.

**Water:** We all have a cool, dispassionate, and reflective capacity that can objectively perceive who or what is before us. Like the reflection on the surface of a still lake, your mind can clearly reflect momentary events, and the truth of your immediate situation. Moment by moment, your inner water element allows you to notice that a stream of thoughts, images, memories, and inner conversations are flashing in the mirror of your mind. Like the fleeting images in a mirror, our thoughts appear and disappear, rising and falling like successive waves.

From time to time, an abrupt flash of clarity might shatter the fog of your inner dialogue, and the familiar meanings and values you've attached to things suddenly drop. You might suddenly see the world as it is rather than as you'd like it to be. This clear vision is the truth of the water element, the cool reflective capacity of mind to see the uniqueness of each experience, creating order out of the jumble of life events. There's a remarkable clarity in how our intellect can capture a comprehensive picture of complex situations.

The water element also appears in the natural world as we notice that there's a brilliance in how water freezes to form crystalline structures, how mist forms droplets on the leaves and branches, mirroring the surrounding world, and how a stream flowing over a flat surface makes everything beneath it transparent, while caressing every nook and cranny of the channel through which it sweeps.

**Earth:** As you settle into your chair, you might have the unmistakable sensation of simply being here. It's the most real thing happening at this moment. Your earthy embodiment allows you to feel solid and grounded. Whether you're experiencing pleasure or pain, your body and its sensory organs reassure you that you're here on this good Earth, experiencing the simplicity of being alive.

Continuing with the practice of silence and stillness, you might become aware of particular sensations and feelings. With nothing standing between you and your felt sense of the moment, your awareness picks up on environmental sounds, lingering fragrances, the aftertaste of your breakfast, or the reassuring substantiality of your animal body. Relating with the energetic aspect of the earth element reveals that the passing experiences of sight, sound, smell, taste, and bodily sensation have a richness and depth you can appreciate. The thrill of embodied life reminds us that we're recipients of the Earth's natural generosity.

The earth element appears in the natural world as luscious landscapes, tropical jungles, the autumnal harvest, and the enduring substantiality of mountains, hills, and human-made structures such as pyramids, castles, and buildings.

**Fire:** As you continue sitting quietly and breathing without effort, you might suddenly become aware that you're drawn to memories of certain people, places, and situations. As you melt the defenses around your heart and belly, you can feel the heat of desire, or the warm radiation of compassion when you think of loved ones. We all have wants and needs, cravings and passions, which thrust us into relationship with the world of others.

Your inner fire generates the magnetic warmth of desire through which you draw the world closer to yourself to be more intimate with it. Communication is happening all the time—as an infant in a stroller coyly smiles at you and melts your heart, or you find yourself longing for cherished times with your now-deceased parents. Feeling into your own fire element, you're enlivened by the warmth and brightness of life itself. The fire element invites communication and emotional connection with the world and restores the spark of attraction with our everyday life. We're irresistibly drawn to life.

**Wind:** The wind element symbolizes the patterns of energy circulating through us and the world, dissolving the boundary between inner and outer and connecting each to each. The same life force spins subatomic particles, propels planets in their elliptical orbits around the sun, and orchestrates the rise and fall of oceanic tides as well as the rhythmic progression of the seasons. You might become giddy as you suddenly realize that you're part of a cosmic dance with no choreographer.

Remarkably, the rhythmic alternation of breath happens without any effort on your part. The cycles of breathing are guided by the same intelligent life force that circulates your blood and regulates the pattern of your heartbeat. You can feel the subtle electricity of life force circulating throughout your mind and body as it gives you an unmistakable feeling of aliveness. Your inner wind allows you to move in new directions and see things from different perspectives. It's also the kinetic force that propels you into action, preparing you for movement toward a specific goal or a particular action, fueling the ambition to fashion a life for yourself.

As you end the meditation, know that you can return to it whenever you want a quick overview of the qualities of each of the five elements.

## How the Book Is Structured

Having gotten a taste of the five elements, you're ready to dive into deeper exploration of each element. The book is divided into five parts, one for each of the elements. The chapters within each section follow a similar sequence.

The opener summarizes key characteristics of each element.

The first chapter in each part allows you to experience the voice of the element speaking directly of its qualities, providing a crystallization of its exalted qualities or gifts.

The next chapter describes the naturally awakened qualities of a particular element.

The following several chapters show how the relationship to the element gets distorted, and describe how the masculine and feminine aspects of the element express themselves.

The succeeding chapter clarifies how each particular element displays itself in your experience in both its exalted and neurotic forms.

The next-to-the-last chapter in each part describes how to transmute the distorted or neurotic aspect of the element into its naturally enlightened form.

In the final chapter for each element, I imagine what Buddha would recommend to help you know each element's gifts experientially, and begin to transform its distorted aspects via specific meditation methods and contemplative practices designed to integrate these energies. These practices will help to clarify when a particular element is dominant in your experience, and how you can best work with both the neurotic and exalted aspects. I encourage you to return to these practices often as you make use of these powerful tools on the left-hand path.

# Part One

# Space Element: Radical Openness and Utter Simplicity

As if peering into the unbounded clear-blue sky, we open into the simplicity of being, where we awaken intuitive wisdom and experience awe and wonder as we connect with the vastness and profundity of the larger universe, within and without.

**Qualities**
Beingness or presence
Nonconceptual wisdom
Openness, trust, innocence
Shadow, ambiguity, uncertainty
Simplicity
Awe and wonder

# 1

# If Space Could Speak

I am the invisible center of your experiential world, the sheer nakedness of every first moment before you shape it into a form and give it a name. I'm the cosmic mother of any and all possibilities, the undefined moment before you have your next thought. Empty of content, I'm the exquisite freshness that's free from your memories and your hope of what the next moment will bring.

Like a centerless circle without beginning or end, I'm the formless atmosphere in which all life unfolds, and where nothing is separate or excluded. Like the still eye of a hurricane I reveal your true identity to be free of struggle or strife, dignified and dynamically still in the midst of life's furious changes. Dare to open to my mysterious nature, and you'll experience a profound knowingness without anything specific needing to be known. Relax deeply into the space within you, and ordinary situations will disclose their hidden side.

With my spacious awareness you'll never exhaust exploring the endless dimensions of yourself, or another, or the most common things in life. Because my wisdom is discovered in the oceanic depths of your mind, I'll always tempt you to step over the familiar boundaries of your known world to taste your inconceivable totality. By placing your trust in my unfathomable wisdom, you'll discover the freedom of spontaneity, playfulness, and creativity where something unexpectedly life-enhancing might occur.

I'm the wisdom of unconditional openness, the enchanting fertile darkness of being itself. I'm the magic of birth and the terror of death. Ignore me at your peril and you'll find yourself spaced out, lost in my immeasurable depth and vastness without direction or relief from confusion.

Yet, by aligning yourself with my spacious nature you'll discover a magnetic pull from your totality that draws your separate parts together into an experience of wholeness. From the mystery of my formlessness, a direction will emerge, lighting the way out of the darkness of confusion and suffering. Won't you dare take a seat in the mystery of my unknowingness?

# 2

# The Open Secret

Einstein famously stated that there are only two ways to live: as though nothing is a miracle, or as though everything is. When we're undefended—psychologically naked, with nothing standing between us and our immediate experience—then everyday miracles are within reach. Opening to the moment unfolding right before our eyes, exactly as it is, becomes a doorway into a magical landscape that awaits our curiosity. It could be the spring rain beating against our windowpane, the texture of the winding gravel road underneath our feet, the smell of freshly cut grass, the lapping of waves along the shore, or the piercing shriek of an infant that shatters the stillness of our morning meditation.

When we're truly open the world meets us in its fullness. When we're not standing outside of this moment as an inner observer, we might feel unreasonably happy, or even burst into tears. Our wide-open engagement with the world transforms it into something unfathomable. The space element is what makes this possible; it's the center of our experiential world, the atmosphere or environment in which our life unfolds in both ecstasy and pain. The first moment of any experience emerges out of neutral psychological space. It might be the precious moment before we're about to say something like "I love you" or "Oh my god!"

The experience of this arising moment can seem uncanny, both inviting and yet threatening. Exploring the refreshing newness of the open moment holds promise, but it can arouse fear because it seems to stretch out beyond our mind's reach, inviting us to step into foreign territory. It's like after having dinner and exchanging details of the day, we and our intimate other might find that we've both run out of things to say. A pause punctuates the space, pregnant with possibility and uncertainty. We might spontaneously reach out to hold our partner's hands as we both gaze wordlessly at each other, not knowing what the next moment will bring. This is the space element, brimming with potential. But can we trust it?

Like the crest of a wave that doesn't break, the space element is always about to take form as one of innumerable possibilities. It's the undefined moment before we have the next thought, image, or memory, or before we express an earthy desire or a heavenly vision. A baby is born to a young couple. They've waited eagerly for this first child and are now filled with wonder as they muse, "Who will this child grow up to be? What will their character be like?" Both parents lean into the mystery of possibility, knowing the outcome is uncertain.

The space element involves this kind of openness and vulnerability. To tap its power and beauty, we need to be okay with the lack of definition that open possibility presents, and with not always having answers. This requires intuitive sensing and trust in the basic friendliness of the universe, in its uncertain yet immense possibilities.

In Buddhist terms, space represents the formless dimension of both ourselves and the cosmos. Space is our authentic nature before it's made manifest in the world of form, like the potential oak tree lying dormant in an acorn, or the potential butterfly in a caterpillar. It's who we are at our depth. The awakened aspect of space is formless wisdom, a knowingness without anything specific being known.

This formlessness is inconceivable to our ordinary way of thinking, which automatically formats our experiences into conceptual categories in order to make sense of them. We tend to do this by dividing our world into the familiar polarities of friend or foe, winners or losers, Democrat or Republican. By staying within the grid of such conceptual categories, we avoid the gray areas, which we've come to believe are threatening because of their ambiguity.

The wisdom energy of space invites us to see that novelty, creativity, and spontaneity emerge from the indistinct, formless margins of life, those areas not mapped out by thought. When we're able to communicate with our inner space, we heighten our sensitivity and receptivity to ordinary situations so that they may disclose their secret or invisible side.

The space element invites us to step over the boundaries and limitations of our habitual ways of seeing the world, so that we can be spontaneous and playful. Space is the exquisite freshness that's free from our memories and our anticipations of what we hope the next moment will bring. An ordinary occasion or situation might suddenly suggest innumerable possibilities that we didn't know existed.

We might awaken into an unplanned Sunday morning and decide to have breakfast alone in an unexplored part of town, or, finding ourselves momentarily unoccupied, we might take delight in our own company. Perhaps having arrived early at an event and finding ourselves without an agenda, we simply drop into the living quality of the moment and discover something poignant about ourselves. When we're not trying to be who or what we imagine we're supposed to be, we might land in the experience we're already having.

As a result the inconceivable benevolence of the universe might suddenly dawn on us with a feeling of deep appreciation for the most ordinary occurrences. Looking out our living-room window we might notice a lone blue jay sitting on a craggy branch, as autumn leaves are swept up in mini-cyclones and rustle in the wind. The hissing of the kettle punctuates the stillness and silence of our room, while the antique Japanese teapot waits faithfully. This atmosphere is palpable and seems to radiate its own brightness. A living spark of *beingness* touches something deep within us, mysteriously evoking our tender appreciation for just this moment, exactly as it is.

What is it about these occasions, both momentary and timeless, that stirs our soul and ignites our imagination? In such moments of radical openness we experience no separation, but rather an uncanny intimacy with the phenomenal world.

# 3

# How Trouble Began in Paradise

In the previous chapter we discussed how the space element promotes an openness, inviting intimacy with and appreciation of the events of everyday life. We might wonder why we don't consistently experience our daily life in this way, why we don't always feel a deep appreciation for our experiences.

According to developmental psychologists we were born with no boundaries in our mind, but just an openness. Beginning with our socialization as infants, we began a process of building boundaries in the natural openness of mind, first separating ourselves from our mother, then from others and from our environment, and eventually separating our mind from our body. As our ego, or sense of self, developed, we lost our connection with the open psychological space with which our life began.

The invisible *me*, sometimes called the "ghost in the machine," is manufactured by our mind as a substitute for our true identity. The ego is the self-conscious part of our mind that stands apart from experience. As such, it doesn't represent our whole being. It can be a useful social convention so that we can refer to ourselves when communicating with others, but it also seduces us into falsely identifying it with our inconceivable totality—with all that we are.

We assume that there's a little *me* inside of our mind sitting in the director's chair commenting, evaluating, judging, and narrating. This assures us that our world is consistent with our beliefs and assumptions. Most of us consider this to be the normal way the mind works, but this inner dialogue creates an artificial barrier between who we take ourselves to be—the invisible person in here—and the rest of the world out there. Consequently, encounters with psychological space may provoke fear, for they reveal that our boundaries aren't as solid as we'd like to believe. The space element temporarily dissolves the border between self and other, revealing our original nature as a radical openness. The experience of openness invites us to step beyond the edges of our known world, but also might threaten us with its formless immensity.

Conditioned by family and culture, we tend to regard the experience of psychological space as an absence, a deficient emptiness. In such boundless moments we can't seem to find ourselves—the *me* we take ourselves to be. Ironically, nothingness threatens the very foundations of who we think we are. So often we try to protect ourselves from the open-endedness of psychological space by filling it, and we succeed in this project by talking to ourselves about what we're experiencing, rather than being *in* it. Perhaps the most pernicious human habit is the continuous subconscious gossip spinning in our head, as we try to make the world fit into our familiar description of it. This separates us from the living quality of experience, causing it to lose its freshness and virgin innocence—the very qualities that the space element makes possible.

Our compulsive inner dialogue marks the great fall from paradise. The apple in the Garden of Eden came from the tree of the knowledge of good and evil. This apple of conceptual knowledge forever cleaved the world into the warring opposites of virtue and sin, beauty and ugliness, work and play. Our continuous loops of inner conversation seem to offer the convincing sense of being a separate self in a world of other separate entities. As we become more sensitive to the tyranny of our ceaseless inner dialogue we might begin to feel mysteriously confined in a prison of our own making, our self-created inner world.

Most of us are so insensitive to this phenomenon that it goes on without notice. It's like going from one room of our home to the other to get a refill of coffee, and finding we've already traveled hundreds of miles in our mind. Perhaps we've thought about our dying aunt in Florida and whether to book a flight to visit her. In the next moment perhaps we've entertained the possibility of getting a dog, but then considered that this would involve moving into a bigger house with a backyard. As our mind begins to take the shape of these concerns, suddenly we remember a dentist appointment tomorrow, and now begin to wonder whether our insurance covers root-canal procedures!

A whole chorus of internal conversations has unraveled as we stepped toward the coffee maker. We weren't present, but lost in space. Our subconscious gossip is the way we fill space in order to buffer ourselves from its challenge to simply open. If we inspect our mind objectively, we might discover that most of our life is spent elsewhere. This disconnection between mind and body is the source of confusion and suffering. Because a distracted mind seems normal, most of us don't recognize that there's a huge contrast between being *here* as opposed to being internally elsewhere. We've learned to hide from ourselves by ignoring the open potential of psychological space.

Ego's secret strategy has been to create a convincing sense of being a *me* inside here, observing the world of otherness, out there. When we stand outside of our experience as an observer, rather than being fully present in it, we convince ourselves of *me*'s independent existence and its continuity through the ravages of change. By solidifying our idea of ourselves we simultaneously solidify the otherwise fluid world of everyday life. We also inadvertently disconnect from the total human being that we are. This creates a psychological abyss, and provokes the great search for substitutes to make us feel whole and complete.

# 4

# The Dark Side of Space

The essence of our inner space element involves the practice of being. This is deceptively simple. We drop into uncharted openness, meeting the world's nakedness with our own. Without holding on to our past or rehearsing for the future, without needing an agenda or map for how to take the next step, we make a spontaneous gesture into the vast landscape of *nowness*. We practice having a fresh take on what seems ordinary, familiar, uninteresting, or even threatening. The wisdom of the space element is trusting in the immense possibilities waiting to be revealed by our awareness.

But there can be a troubling shadowy aspect to the open moment. The ambiguity of things that have multiple dimensions, shifting meanings, and unpredictable outcomes can turn our ordered world on its head. Our need to come to conclusions, to finalize our thoughts and feelings about specific people and situations, is perhaps threatened by life's unpredictable open-endedness. We can never really exhaust all there is to know or experience about another or ourselves, nor can we ever hit bottom to discover a final, incontrovertible truth. And every relationship ultimately remains incomplete, imperfect, and uncertain.

When a loved one confesses that they're not sure about their relationship with us, we can be thrown into the amorphous space of uncertainty. Everything in us wants to dispel the formless ambiguity so that our world can resume its predictable and familiar shape and we can feel safe again. But a more daring gesture might be to stay with the uncertainty until it reveals something about ourselves or our relationship that we were avoiding. Such a gesture lends weight and substance to our character.

Exploring the inner space of our own being we often stumble across strange feelings and images, long-forgotten memories, and primitive desires, which can make us feel uncertain about who we really are. To be intimate with our interior as if it were a lover means that no thought, image, or feeling can be regarded as alien. As the poet Rilke suggested, we have to learn to love everything strange within ourselves. This aspect of the space element can be very challenging because of our habitual tendency to insist that friend and enemy be kept clearly defined and separate.

The willingness to experience shadowy feelings and alien aspects of ourselves carves out a sanctuary within our soul where light and shadow, friend and enemy, and conscious and unconscious can coexist. Paradoxically, this radical embrace permits us to be more at home in the world, more forgiving of those who are different, more accepting of what is deformed or broken, and more tolerant of life's ambiguity.

The seemingly uneventful and insignificant intervals between home and work, between waiting in line at the ATM and shopping at the market, can drop us into mindless oblivion. Driven by the momentum of our busy life, so often we don't pay attention to these in-between places. With our attention focused on the next destination, we inadvertently space out from what's presently unfolding, placing ourselves at a distance from the immediacy of situations.

When a gap or interval unexpectedly opens in the middle of the day, or when the world confronts us with what we weren't expecting—like when a plan falls through or a relationship abruptly changes its tone—we come face-to-face with the groundlessness of our life. The rawness of not knowing what's next can either trigger our survival anxiety or serve as a catalyst. Perhaps we could pause in the openness of the unknown and intuitively sense the pregnant potential of the moment.

When we take our first step out the door in the morning, rather than give in to our subconscious gossip and daily preoccupations, we might open and abruptly shift our attention to look at the morning with fresh eyes. Imagine seeing a brilliant marigold that's blooming through a crack in a broken fence as an iridescent monarch butterfly zigzags through the air. Are we truly separate from the marigold and the butterfly who have found a place within us? Can we actually find a boundary where the marigold and the butterfly end and our visual consciousness begins? In our vivid perceptions do we not discover ourselves in them?

Because each moment is undetermined and without absolute boundaries, there's no limit to what we can appreciate about any person or thing or experience. When we fully appreciate anyone or anything, we're not insisting that the world be any different than it is. At such precious moments we're fully aligned with life, and relieved of the burden of separation and struggle.

# 5

# The Space Element's Personal Touch

When we experience the space element directly instead of through the filter of ego, or our idea of ourselves, it conveys a sense of ultimate value and meaning. The wisdom energy of space is the awakened quality of radical openness and infinite possibility that inspires awe and wonder. Communicating with the space element involves a deep trust in life's goodness, which permits us to momentarily drop whatever we're holding to meet the world with neither our habitual patterns of defense nor an agenda about how we want or expect things to be.

The space element is our gift for intuitive awareness, our power to know something directly and immediately without having to think about it or use reason or evidence to reach a conclusion. With intuitive awareness we're able to tune into *being* itself. When we do this we can realize that our fundamental worth or basic goodness doesn't have to be earned. Being *is* the depth of who we are. When we touch this dimension of ourselves with awareness, we sense that we belong to the world, and that we have as much validity as a tree, or a mountain, or a star.

Like the formlessness of space that has no boundaries and includes everything within its scope, when the space element is dominant in our personality we can intuitively realize we are connected with all things and beings. As we become intimate with our inner space, we experience a basic goodness or worthiness at our core, known as *bodhicitta* in Sanskrit, and realize that our participation in life is necessary for the greater good. Embodying the energy of basic goodness we can function in alignment with our environment rather than feeling that we're shaped and conditioned by it. We now feel empowered to respond to our genuine needs and wants, and our behavior is no longer a sacrificial effort to accommodate others.

Like the simplicity of space itself we manifest as a peaceful presence and allow situations to unfold naturally. This simplicity includes a flexibility and receptivity to contradictory perspectives and diverse ways of being. Our comfort with uncertainty and ambiguity creates an atmosphere where conflicting opinions are valued, so that no one feels excluded and where everyone can find their own voice.

The distortion of the space element begins with our misinterpretation of our inner space as a deficient emptiness, the feeling that something is lacking in us. We tend to disconnect from the depths of our own interior and compensate for this loss by trying to replicate the qualities of space, but in a contorted way. We narrow our awareness and numb our sensitivities as if trying to mimic the imperturbability of space.

When we're under the influence of the space element, we tend to feel indistinct, featureless, and without protective boundaries, much like space itself. Having disconnected from the wisdom energy of space, we might conclude that we're insignificant and without distinction or uniqueness, lacking in qualities that could earn recognition and love from others.

Although this estrangement from our essential nature is common whenever we're out of alignment with any of the elements, when our relationship with the space element is distorted, we feel this most acutely. Thinking of ourselves as uninteresting, bland, or generic—like empty space—we might doubt whether there's a good reason to explore ourselves or our world. Such exploration might threaten us with the recognition that parts of our life demand change, which would ruffle the buffered, formless quality of our manufactured sense of space. Since our basic motivation is to avoid rocking the boat, rousing inquisitiveness seems to require too much effort. In the neurotic state, we might prefer to remain in a cognitive fog, where nothing is very defined or demanding, as we find comfort in a kind of psychospiritual sleep or inertia.

Like space itself, which has no center but is all-pervasive, when we have a distorted relationship with our inner space element we might easily merge with the external environment in order to promote ease and comfort. Blending with other people's wishes or our company's agenda offers the consolation of connection, but causes a loss of communication with our inner world. Forgetting our own priorities by going along with what others want prevents us from discovering what we truly want and need.

The inertia of space manifests as being overly adaptable, compromising, and self-sacrificing in relationships, preferring to blend in rather than stand out. When our relationship with inner space becomes neurotic, we seek emotional homeostasis in order to minimize any disturbance to our billowy, cloudlike comfort. By living at a distance from our inner depths, we tend to be disconnected from our body and our instincts. We usually don't assert any position of our own because of our unconscious sense of deficiency and unworthiness. Due to our numbing and dumbing-down strategy, no one thing or quality stands out as being particularly important to provoke a strong response from us, and so we secretly avoid conflict or challenge. We've converted the natural sense of openness and simplicity of our inner space by filling it with substitute pleasures and inessential activities.

Eventually we may be gripped by a double conflict, between our desire to accommodate other people's wishes and our desire to assert our authenticity, and the conflict between our wish to remain socially invisible and our suppressed desire for recognition. If we're willing to face these conflicts and cut through our inertia, we come face-to-face with our demons. We're now ready to confront our defensive habit of spacing out, which has led to a kind of spiritual laziness. As we journey into our own psychological abyss, the indistinct, foglike quality that enabled us to ignore the details of our life begins to lift. We realize that our penchant for spacing out was the negative version of being or presence—the capacity to simply be.

As we recognize that our habit of ignoring was a strategy to hide from life's challenges, deficient emptiness can morph into the wisdom energy of space. Our habitual tendency to disconnect from our instinctual nature is gradually transformed into a grounded sense of bodily presence and vitality.

From the perspective of the left-hand teachings, our neurotic patterns can become protectors when they remind us to bring awareness to whatever limits our Buddha nature.

# 6

# Befriending the Demon of Space

The demon or shadow side of the space element presents itself as ambiguity, uncertainty, tentativeness, or groundlessness. It often manifests as the fear of losing ourselves, becoming overwhelmed by the specter of too much possibility, too much openness, without definition or guidelines. We tend to space out from the fluid, unpredictable quality of the open moment through the self-forgetfulness of our inner dialogue.

Creative communication with the demon of the space element uncovers its message—what it really wants from us. We might discover that our ritualistic behaviors and obsessions around money, food, and sex have to do with not knowing how to relate with simplicity or how to make use of boredom—the threat of the blank canvas. When we encourage ourselves to recognize that the demon's outward neurotic pattern is made of the same substance as Buddha nature, only then does the wisdom of space sparkle through.

The left-hand path demonstrates that there's no area of experience that does not radiate the wisdom energy of Buddha nature. When we become intimate with the demon's energy, it offers the opportunity for confusion to dawn as wisdom, as we see clearly how we've used confusion to postpone having to initiate change or make a necessary decision.

The left-hand path teaches us to cultivate openness so that when either pleasant or unpleasant experiences arise, we stay close to their energy in order to be intimate with what's unfolding at the moment. This awareness marches us into the territory that most of us flee from—the immediate experience we're already having!

When we catch ourselves compulsively cleaning or spacing

out when we have to make a difficult decision, or spending hours on Facebook when we'd be better off sleeping, we abruptly flash on openness. We might discover that we're experiencing anxiety or boredom, or an aching emptiness. By refusing to reinforce the compelling neurotic pattern that has us in its grip, we transform our demons into protectors, who heighten our awareness of what we're doing and what function our patterns serve.

We might notice that ignoring our own interior has permitted us a superficial sense of inner peace. Perhaps our patterns of avoidance have prevented us from integrating the pieces of our life that could give us a clear and coherent image of ourselves. As we learn to trust in what's difficult, we might recognize that our disturbing feelings and repetitious behavioral patterns want our love and acceptance, not defensiveness and negative judgment.

In order to transform demons into protectors, we need to relax our opposition to their energy. The first step is to drop the narrative we may have been associating with a problematic feeling or behavioral pattern. Second, we inquire whether the pattern or its energy suggests something to us. Third, we inquire whether we're willing to truly listen, or whether we're becoming defensive and filtering the message. Last, if we're becoming defensive, we bring our attention to the wall that separates us from the feelings, impulses, or images that are restricting our attention. What are we resisting? What are we so reluctant to feel or to recognize? What are the consequences of our denial?

Spirituality happens in the life we're already living and not in some transcendent realm. Demons become protectors when we empower them to remind us that we can't hide from the wholeness of ourselves, which includes order and chaos, neurosis and sanity. Recognizing the all-inclusive wisdom of space, we get an unforgettable glimpse of the interconnectedness of all things and beings. We're more likely to accept pleasure and pain, sadness and joy, aloneness and togetherness, without having to keep them separate in order to feel safe. The demons of self-forgetfulness, uncertainty, and inertia might expose our belief that to be connected with others we thought we had to sacrifice connection with ourselves.

Imagine that while having dinner at a favorite neighborhood restaurant, someone at the next table smiles knowingly at us. Uncertain what to do next, we reciprocate by smiling reflexively. We're not sure whether this person knows us and we've forgotten who they are, or whether they're simply a friendly patron, or if something about them genuinely provokes our interest. Should we permit ourselves to become inquisitive about this individual or get busy eating our dinner? Establishing a relationship with the space element suggests that we take a few seconds to experience our vulnerability—our discomfort with uncertainty and lack of definition—before proceeding with our dinner. There's no formula for doing the right thing.

By staying curious about what arises, keeping our ears and eyes and our heart open, we might change our idea of this person, or ourselves. To work creatively with the space element entails sensitively attuning ourselves to the energy of relationships and events as they're unfolding, so that we can paradoxically both go along with and yet influence their movement. We learn to honor our own preferences as well as the actual situations and events of daily life.

When we're willing to be fully present in the gap, in the tentativeness of not knowing, we might notice an opening—a neutral space that spontaneously appears—providing us an unusual opportunity. In this opening we can ride the possibilities that space offers us.

In the midst of our everyday activities, we might suddenly become aware that this neutral space manifests as a sense of presence. We simply take a moment to be in silence and stillness, enjoying the profound simplicity of the unfolding moment. Such a lack of struggle promotes a feeling of being there all at once, an unmistakable sense of wholeness. The openness of space *is* our own vivid awareness, which is wise beyond reason. It inspires us to feel the grace of our human existence, the miracle of being, which can only be realized *now*, and *now* again.

When we dare to communicate with what is formless, we can relax into unbounded openness, an uncommon world where light and dark, inside and outside, self and other, have no quarrel with each other. There are no strangers in this world because no experience is judged as alien. Whether pleasurable or painful, through gain or loss, praise or blame, whatever we experience belongs to the ever-changing landscape that is our unique life journey.

Contrary to the commonsense notion that something can't come out of nothing, everything we experience comes out of nothing, the fertile openness of space. As if streaming through an invisible source, an inexhaustible point, the natural world of "ten thousand things" is re-created moment by moment. We're never separate from this inexhaustible source, which is the wisdom energy of the space element. It's ultimately who we are at our depth.

The left-hand path reminds us that exactly as we are, with all of our neuroses, with all of our dysfunctional patterns, we're an eccentric expression of primordial intelligence, or Buddha nature. We don't have to throw away or sanitize our neuroses or take spiritual detergent and cleanse ourselves to make our transcendental sanity or Buddha nature shine. Our neurotic expression is displaying Buddha nature but in a distorted fashion. Exactly as we are, with all our imperfections and quirks, we're a unique expression of the universe's story. We're always safe within our experience.

# 7

# What Buddha Might Recommend

This chapter invites a direct experience of the space element through meditation and contemplative practices. Engaging in these practices allows the material to come alive and begins the process of allowing yourself to receive its gifts.

## Space Element Meditation

Take a comfortably seated position, and remain in silence and stillness for ten to fifteen minutes. Encourage yourself not to become preoccupied with any concerns. As if peering into a cloudless sky, simply be with your experience of bare openness. When either past or future thoughts kidnap your attention, just bring yourself back to the sense of presence, allowing yourself to just *be*. When you notice that you're thinking, immediately release any thoughts or images, and return your attention to your physical presence or the natural cycle of your breathing.

If you find you're experiencing a pain in your knee, hunger pangs in your stomach, or feeling pleasantly lightheaded, then be fully present with these sensations, letting go of any judgment or story you might have about them. You're giving yourself permission to be as you are without trying to improve yourself or explain anything to yourself. It's very important to be kind and compassionate by not judging yourself negatively when you do get carried away. Remind yourself that this is a human problem, not yours alone.

## Practical Applications

*Everyday life*
At any moment of the day when you don't have to be somewhere

and don't have to perform some task, abruptly become aware that *this* is a moment of openness. Try to relax into it, if only momentarily. Simply be with this immediate moment without giving it a name or form, without needing to have a direction or purpose. Refrain from shaping the formlessness of the moment by defining it or by trying to make it fit your beliefs. In this way you reconnect with the wisdom of space in everyday life.

### Shadow inquiry
The space element includes the nonconscious aspects of our mind. We can become conscious of these hidden areas through inquiry. Either work with a trusted partner or, if you prefer to work alone, journal your process.

(A) Begin by asking either your partner or yourself, "May I speak with the part of you/myself that's weak, cowardly, guilty, wounded, naive, deceptive, sneaky, or dependent [the so-called inferior aspects—the hidden or shadow parts that embarrass or humiliate you] so that it may find its own voice?" You might ask this part of yourself what it wants to say to you. You could respond and initiate a dialogue with your shadow. If working alone, write out what this aspect of yourself is saying.

Notice whether you're negatively judging or resisting the shadowy aspect of yourself. Such judgment or resistance usually takes the form of not being willing to acknowledge or communicate with the inferior aspects of yourself. The point of this contemplative process is to open to your intrinsic wholeness, which includes light and shadow. It's essential to allow the shadow aspect to speak without inhibition, so encourage yourself to morph fully into that aspect of yourself.

(B) Imagine if your shadow were an actual person. What would they look like? What kind of life would they be living? Describe this figure in detail, using your journal if you're working alone.

Inquire whether you could be friends with such a person. What would the quality of that friendship be like? If not, explore your own resistance or rejection of this person.

(C) Ask your partner or yourself, "May I speak with the dimension of yourself/myself that's wise, caring, compassionate, strong, mature, appreciative, and beautiful [or any other positive quality that you usually don't acknowledge]?" Then allow this part to speak so it can discover its own voice. You could question this positive aspect of yourself and ask why you have difficulty embracing its qualities. If this spiritual double were an actual person, what would they look like? What kind of life would they be living?

Many of us suppress the aspect of ourselves that's basically good, compassionate, and wise—the dimension of ourselves that's deeply spiritual. Ironically, this becomes part of our shadow.

### Inquiry into nonbeing or death

One of the most difficult yet rewarding aspects of working with the space element is opening to nonbeing or psychological death. Space is radical openness, the absence of all the familiar reference points by which we define ourselves. It's the last thing we want to open to because from the ego's point of view it feels like suicide. Yet, for a caterpillar to be reborn as a butterfly, it completely lets go of its caterpillarness before it can embrace its new life as a butterfly.

In this contemplation, we're permitting ourselves to get a real sense of the freedom and the threat of letting go. Contemplate your own necessary mortality by progressively letting go of all the reference points that define you and your world. Death marks the end of your connection with family, friends, and cherished places, the end of everything and everyone you love and value. You no longer experience the simple enjoyments of life, such as sleeping, eating, good conversation, and making love. Gone is the deep-blue sky, the sound of rain on your windows, the smell of freshly cut grass, the delightful feeling of your loved one snuggling with you.

Work with a partner or journal in solitude. For short periods of time, practice saying goodbye to and then expressing gratitude for every aspect of your life. Include the gifts of sight, sound, smell, taste, and touch, the capacity to think and to love, as well as every valued relationship and every precious connection with your world.

After each period of doing this practice, ask yourself how the contemplation of dying has affected the quality of your life, your interpersonal relationships, and your sense of reverence and gratitude.

# Part Two

# Water Element:
# Reflective Clarity and Unbiased Perception

Like images mirrored on the surface of a still lake, we reflect our world clearly and precisely without the distorting influence of discursive thought, awakening our mind's natural brilliance to form a comprehensive view of life.

**Qualities**
Transparency
Clarity, brilliance
Inquisitiveness
Discernment
Unbiased perception
Capacity for flowing

# 8

# If Water Could Speak

I am the mind's capacity for reflection, which enables you to emerge from your invisible center into visibility. My power of mirrorlike awareness enables you to objectively see yourself as well as the things of your everyday world. I'm the first sense of yourself as a visible form, and also the first perception of the world as *other*, as distinct from yourself.

Like a clear mirror, I reflect every nuance, every facet, of situations as part of one seamless whole. I cut through your conceptualized version of things to reveal the world as *it is*, not as you would like it to be. Like an indestructible diamond I cut through confusion and ambiguity to illuminate who or what is before you, before your personal narrative muddies the waters.

My continuous movement disrupts your fixed pattern of thoughts, and therefore I evade all definition. Because of my shape-shifting flowing current I can evoke lightninglike flashes of insight, and dissolve your solid image of yourself and others into fluidity.

I can take the form of liquid, vapor, or solid ice, revealing the fluid nature of mind as a stream of consciousness, and as the source of imagination as it transforms one thing into another. My watery energy has an empathic quality and can also mirror others in an emotional way, reflecting back to them what they're feeling.

My virtue lies in cutting through what is confused and indistinct to reveal a crystal-clear and undistorted image of reality. This capacity is what allows you to establish a panoramic and coherent view of your own life. If you're foolish enough to disconnect from me, you exile yourself to the tower of your mind, where you'll observe life at a distance. Having fallen into the trap of looking at surface images rather than what underlies appearances, you'll tend to boycott your feelings in favor of thinking, and maintain emotional distance to prevent the danger of intimacy.

However, if you dare to join with me, then, like a bubbling brook or waterfall, my energy will elicit a spirit of playful fluidity and celebration, preventing your life from becoming frozen in endless conceptualization and ingrained routines and habitual patterns.

# 9

# The Ocean Inside Us

Consider the natural element of water. Our body is comprised of nearly 70 percent fluid. Tears drop, flow, roll, trickle, or gush down our cheeks in both sadness and joy. Bodily fluid flows as blood through our arteries and veins, carrying oxygen and nutrients to every cell of our body. Bodily liquid swirls and swishes, removing toxins, lubricating our joints, and moistening the tissues of our mouth, eyes, and nose. Water transports essential chemicals to our heart and brain, while flushing out waste products from our kidneys and liver.

Water also flows, merges, and yields, joining us to what we want and those who we love. Imagine holding the trembling hand of our aged grandmother as she looks lovingly at us, our inner water dissolving the artificial membrane that separates youth from age, as we enter her fragile world, surrendering the immunity of our youth. Typically we armor ourselves against such merger experiences.

Our inner water element is highly receptive to impressions, mirroring who or what is before us. Like the pristine reflection on the surface of a still lake, our mind can clearly reflect the truth of our situation, undisturbed by the winds of desire or anticipation, hope or fear.

Imagine sitting before a beautiful alpine lake surrounded by lush meadows. The wind is blowing across the surface of the lake, transforming the sunlight into swirling orbs of sparkling light. Nothing of the surrounding environment is reflected clearly. The play of light excites our imagination as we project all kinds of ideas and images, and memories and associations, onto the lake's surface. Later in the afternoon when the wind stops blowing, the very same lake now reveals a perfect mirrorlike image of the surrounding alpine forest. The image is so pristine that it's hard to tell the actual landscape from its reflection. Our inner dialogue with our mind's tangential thinking is analogous to the wind blowing over the surface of the lake. Unknowingly, we project our preconceptions, expectations, assumptions, and value judgments — our personal narrative — onto the clear surface of reality.

The familiar and predictable sense of ourselves — the small *me* — is the part of the mind that is commonly called the ego. Its strategy is to convert our life into a protective cocoon that gives us a convincing feeling of safety and security. Our continuously running inner dialogue and our habitual patterns prevent shocks and surprises to our known world. This personal narrative of hopes and fears, desires and fantasies, plans and agendas, is what we project onto otherwise neutral situations. Like spiders, we tend to spin a web around the bare skeleton of the world, made up of our remembered history and our anticipated future, so that the world takes on a very familiar appearance.

The uninspected life occurs when we look but don't see, listen but don't hear, touch but don't feel. The problem is that the overlapping layers of our inner conversations, and the monotony of our everyday routines, have kidnapped our childlike sense of wonder. The world is no longer enchanted for us! Our perceptions can become so blunted that we may be sleepwalking through our days in a largely distracted state. Most of the time we may be elsewhere, going through the motions, but not actually living in the moment unfolding right before our eyes.

Yet, when we tune into the wisdom energy of our inner water element, we discover that we have a cool, dispassionate, and reflective capacity to objectively perceive who or what is before us in intricate detail. Perhaps we notice that there's a brilliance in how icicles hang from branches, how windowpanes frost over in paisley patterns, and how raindrops striking a puddle create perfect concentric circles. Seeing the uniqueness of each experience, especially in the midst of repetitious activity, is the art of the left-hand approach to everyday life.

In the Buddhist mandala, the water element is associated with the east, the direction of the rising sun, which brings the dawning of each new day. Illuminating the landscape by making trees, rocks, streams, and grazing animals visible, the east represents the first light and the sense of sight and insight. The reflectiveness of water symbolizes a mirrorlike awareness of both ourselves and the things of our everyday world. This is our innate capacity for direct perception, a clear seeing of who or what is before us without overlaying our personal story or belief system onto people or daily events.

Whereas the space element suddenly opens us up into a wordless atmosphere of stillness and silence, our inner water brilliantly reflects the details of what is there without distortion. On a morning walk with our dog along a lovely country road, we might be traveling on a different trail as our mind jumps from thoughts about tonight's dinner to this afternoon's dentist appointment, from anticipating a difficult meeting with our boss to images of an upcoming vacation with our family. We barely notice the lush landscape in which our dog is fully immersed.

Yet, our water element can abruptly awaken us from our sleepwalking, perhaps at the sight of a snow-white egret knee-deep in a dark-green pond, poised like a samurai ready to strike at the faintest stirring. Such direct and immediate perception is uncanny. Through the encounter with the egret, the visible other, separate and different from ourselves, we meet our invisible self. The egret arises within us, at once enriching our experience of the world but also bringing us face-to-face with ourselves.

When the clouds of our rambling, tangential thoughts part, ordinary things or events shine with uncommon brilliance. We might suddenly find ourselves looking at someone or something without names or familiar descriptions, without the history that we've attached to that person or thing. Such crystal-clear reflection has a shocking freshness and crispness, delivering us to this moment from which nothing is missing. The wisdom energy of water helps us break free from our narrow ways of thinking to realize that the ordinary world is its own work of art.

# 10

# Feminine and Masculine Aspects of Water

A stream's fluidity expresses water's feminine capacity of receptivity as it caresses every nook and cranny of the channel through which it sweeps. Ever changing and yielding, neither resisting nor grasping what it meets, water makes intimate contact with everything within its currents while remaining transparent. Whereas the masculine quality of water represents clear and precise reflection, the feminine capacity for movement prevents such clear perception from becoming frozen like a still photo. The feminine brings a dynamic quality to the water's still reflection so that, moment by moment, we can experience fresh perceptions, and not get caught in holding rigidly to our fixed ideas and images.

Imagine that on a visit with our aging parents, our father begins what appears to be his predictable rant about "the liberals," which causes us to feel both irritated and emotionally flat. At that very moment our feeling of being stuck could be a catalyst to notice the animation in our father's eyes and the vigor of his gestures. Without tuning out of his conversation we might reflect upon how our father has strong convictions and is willing to fight for what he believes is right. We recognize that his repeated desire to share this part of himself with us may be his way of showing us that he both loves us and wants our love.

The feminine quality of our inner water element is our capacity to flow gently into the heart and mind of another when we're invited to do so, and emotionally or psychologically mirror them, reflecting and affirming what they're experiencing. Listening not only with our ears but with our heart, our watery nature can nurture or merge with others with empathic sensitivity.

The feminine quality of water is embodied in the Chinese

principle of the endlessly flowing *Tao*, whose fluidity evades all definition, having the power to dissolve our fixed image of ourselves and the world into formlessness. The effortless grace by which nature expresses herself reflects a lack of forced effort. In one respect, the Tao symbolizes the fluid and elegant nature of mind as a stream of consciousness. We can experience this fluidity when we meditate, as we witness the endless waves of thoughts and images emerging and dissolving into the sea of our awareness.

Our inner water element can take the form of liquid, vapor, or solid ice, which suggests our power to shape-shift, and to creatively transform our life. The feminine aspect of water, reflecting our mind's capacity for movement and change, can create sudden surprises, and the unexpected breakup of things we thought were solid and unchangeable. The water element is also the creative impulse to spill over boundaries and initiate fresh beginnings—perhaps when it suddenly occurs to us to leave a relationship or a job in which we've felt trapped for years.

The masculine water element is undistorted clarity, the analytical and conceptual approach to experience. Its undistracted and undistorted perception, transparent and brilliant, surveys an entire area and clearly mirrors the ever-changing field of vision. It is also crisp and sharp like jagged ice, which cuts through what's confused and indistinct, revealing a crystal-clear image of reality.

The Greek god Apollo provides an apt metaphor for the masculine quality of water. He's the embodiment of emotionally cool observation at a distance. He's very much at home in the sky realm of mind and is known for his clarity, but also for his remoteness and unapproachability. Apollo sees clearly from afar, observing the details of life from an aerial perspective. He has a bias for clear definitions, preferring to look at surface images rather than at what underlies appearances. He favors thinking over feeling, distance over closeness, and objective analysis over subjective intuition. His perception is uncolored by his emotions, a useful quality when, for example, a parent needs to set a difficult limit or boundary for their child.

The masculine power of the abstract intellect can form a comprehensive view of complex situations, clarifying the relationship among and between individual forms. For instance, instead of perceiving only an individual nose, mouth, and jaw, eyes and head, we recognize a human face. Suddenly, segments of our life that have felt like scattered jigsaw pieces come together in a flash of insight, revealing a coherent image of things as they truly are, and perhaps suggesting a way forward. Our resentment at not having a voice in our marriage, the lack of recognition from our superiors at work, and our father's reluctance to affirm our choice of a career might all suddenly come together to reveal our own doubt and hesitation to shine our spirit in such a way that others can feel it.

When we bring the undistorted clarity of masculine reflection into relationship with the flowing and receptive quality of the feminine, we experience more balance and harmony in our life. We see things precisely as they are, not only physically but with awareness of their spiritual significance. For instance, one of water's properties is cohesion, its natural power to form drops. The membrane that holds water to a circular shape is due to molecular attraction, which unites water into cohesive units. One implication of this capacity is that our inner water element doesn't simply mirror the many aspects of our life like snapshots but spontaneously integrates the seeming randomness of events into coherent wholes.

The frustration we felt with our spouse after an early-morning conversation, the disappointment we experienced after an interaction with our teenage daughter, and the self-criticism that we leveled at ourselves lead to a realization that all of these were based on our ancient belief that if we can't do things perfectly then we're not worthy of love or respect.

When we overemphasize water's masculine aspect of crystal clarity, we become biased in wanting things to always be clear, orderly, and precise. When we recognize our bias, we try to integrate the feminine energy of flow into our experience to include feelings of vulnerability, uncertainty, and tenderness. Acknowledging our imperfections and our lack of understanding about many things in life cuts through the fear of making mistakes. This feminine quality of receptivity returns us to our body's natural rhythms and the fluidity of our sensations and feelings.

When we emphasize water's feminine qualities we might find ourselves overly receptive and yielding, as we fail to resist what demands to be resisted. At that moment such an experience can be a catalyst to integrate the masculine principle of water. Water's cohesiveness eliminates extraneous distractions and seductions to provide a protective boundary to keep safe what's precious, what's integral to our unique personhood. The membrane that holds water as drops symbolizes the wisdom of the water element, the undistorted clarity that helps us preserve a personal sense of integration and coherence despite a stream of disjointed experiences.

When we're choicelessly aware, unlimited in our willingness to be both precise and fluid, crystal-clear and yielding, then like a bubbling brook or waterfall everyday life can be an expression of our deep appreciation for the vividness and dynamism of the most ordinary things.

# 11

# Distortions of Everyday Life

Some of us may be old enough to remember the movie theaters we went to as children where someone operated a mechanical projector in a small booth in the back of the theater. A huge strip of celluloid containing still photos was rapidly spun around on a metal spool as a brilliant bulb projected these illuminated images onto the movie screen. Like magic, a convincing illusion was created of characters moving, talking, and taking part in an unfolding drama. We might've cried or despaired, laughed or rejoiced, as we and our parents became absorbed in the story.

Metaphorically, the projector bulb is analogous to awareness itself, our capacity for cognitive radiance. The celluloid photos represent the thoughts we spin from our inventory of memories, beliefs, desires, expectations, and value judgments. The blank screen symbolizes the situations as they actually are before we dress them up with our projections. The projector bulb has no bias toward what it illuminates, but simply projects whichever photos are presented to it.

The grand distortion of everyday life is our cherished belief that the world is exactly as we imagine it. Most of us don't realize that we assemble the world according to our learned description of it, overlaying it with our projections, and then behave as if the world actually possessed our judgments, conflicts, expectations, hopes, and fears. This disparity between situations as they are and our subjective version of them is the primary cause of confusion and conflict.

The Sanskrit term *samsara* refers to the mechanism of the wheel, our motivation to compulsively spin it, and the collective repository of all of our psychic inventory. All too often the result of spinning samsara's wheel is that we want what we can't get, or get what we don't want, or finally we get whom or what we thought we wanted only to find out that we're still hungry. We seem to be perpetually on the move to find a better moment than the one we're already in.

According to Buddhist psychology, the continual effort to solidify a self who stands out and apart from our experiences disconnects us from the experience of wholeness, that unmistakable sense of being of one piece. The core fear associated with the water element is the feeling that we, the separate self, are isolated, alone within our own consciousness and bound by our skin-encapsulated body. We feel cut-off from the wellspring of life, disconnected from our own body and its feelings, intuitions, and emotional depths.

Water neurosis fears that the penetrating clarity and sharpness of raw experience will pierce our protective armor and that we'll find ourselves painfully visible. For example, when we feel that we've been seen and we're not ready to be seen, even by ourselves, we tend to push away or attack anyone who makes us feel too transparent and vulnerable. The thought of being penetrated by truths that we're not ready to receive provokes us to defend ourselves by intellectualizing our experiences, which keeps us emotionally distant from threatening situations or people.

What we call *mind* extends beyond our skin-encapsulated body and brain to include the surrounding world. Our waterlike mind isn't situated apart from the jasmine it reflects, but includes the reflected entity as part of itself. We participate in the jasmine vine's *isness*. The things and beings of our world ask us to be intimate with them so that they may come to life through us.

Trees and meadows, the bubbling brook and the hazy moon, our children playing and our cat yawning—all come into existence as they're reflected in our awareness. Like a clear mirror, we can reflect every nuance, every aspect, and every dimension of a situation to reveal the many separate details of both our internal world and the surrounding environment, recognizing both inner and outer as a seamless whole.

It's like dancing with a partner and being fully involved. There's only the heightened awareness of the flow of dancing. It's one field of movement and awareness without a clearly defined sense of inside and outside. Conversely, we might be at a funeral service for a loved one and surrender to our feelings of grief. Our loving memory of our friend, the funeral service, and our grief are part of the same vivid stream.

We discover the water element's magic in our fluid awareness, which reflects our world far and wide as well as near and deep. Such flowing awareness elicits a spirit of playfulness and a feeling of delight and discovery, which prevents our life from becoming a frozen pattern of projections. Living in such an undivided state permits us to be both totally ourselves and fully in the world, even during times of bitter disappointment, sadness, and loneliness.

# 12

# Fearing Our Own Depths

As water conforms to the shape of the container into which it's poured, likewise our internal water element has shaped itself to fit within the boundaries of our family and culture. We've been conditioned to structure our experience in ways that conform to the beliefs and expectations of our family, milieu, and culture. The capacity to conform is both a problem and a promise.

This quality of water speaks to our ability to gain membership in our society and to creatively adapt to changing circumstances. At the same time, our tendency to shape ourselves in conformity with the social agreements of society often conflicts with our need to be our own person, to be truly ourselves. Most of us live with the tension between conformity and rebellion, between maintaining a social image and hungering to explore the inner depths beneath it—a thorny proposition.

We have fashioned a social face, or *persona*, to present to the world, but behind our social presentation lie our hidden depths. These depths include the dimension of ourselves that transcends our egoic identity and our culture. As a result, it's as if we, the creators of the persona, have become afraid of our own watery depths because of what they may reveal. Many of us have cultivated a preference for thinking over deep feeling, and emotional distance over intimacy. Surprises and revelations that threaten our persona or self-image usually trigger fear, causing us to feel bewildered and defensive.

A pervasive cultural belief tells us that feelings could be dangerous because they take us to depths where we're no longer in control and where we could be disadvantaged. Although it may seem safer and more prudent to think rather than feel, in so doing we lose contact with the gritty earthiness of situations.

In other words, by separating our head from both our heart and our belly, we exile ourselves to living in a realm of abstraction, having little skin in the game.

This hidden aspect of the water element is the reflex to withhold ourselves from fully participating in life and instead to live in the tower of mind. We may be like someone who lives alone in a castle surrounded by a large moat, preferring to spend our time in the tower, where we have a panoramic perspective of the surrounding towns and villages. From time to time we may get lonely and emotionally cold, and hunger for stimulation, contact, and communication with others.

Periodically, we come down from the tower, lower the drawbridge, cross over the moat, and venture forth onto land where we interact with others and engage in the social activities of the village. However, we eventually become saturated with the thrill of new sensations—the impress of colors, forms, fragrances, and compelling conversations—and begin to long for the serene stillness of our tower. We begin to pull back emotionally and soon withdraw to our castle, returning to the tower and its exalted perspective, where we can reflect upon our experiences in the stillness of solitude, now far from the madding crowd.

The mind's capacity for abstraction and analytic thinking can create a complex net of ideas and images. Although such reflection can be elegant and capture the overarching principles of a situation, it can disconnect us from our own body and cut us off from the wellspring of life. This split can lead to the distortion that our awareness is trapped within our skull rather than flowing through us and connecting us with everything.

The mirrorlike quality of the water element includes more than visual images. It's the synthesizing capacity of the intellect to continually "story" our experiences, transforming them into our subjective version of life. We might finesse people, places, and things into our narrative to provide justification for our peculiar perspective on life. In such a highly personalized reflection of the world, we're often unaware that we're living more in our story than in the actual world.

When this happens, it's as if we've made a bargain with the devil. We begin to justify and rationalize everything in terms of our pseudological system, filtering out inconvenient facts in order to make things fit our idiosyncratic system. Increasingly disconnected from feeling and instinct, heart and belly, we may adopt a personal philosophy or outlook that resists anything that would contradict or challenge our story, but we find ourselves repeatedly threatened by these very themes.

Staying within the safe and predictable margins of our personal narrative reinforces the descriptions we hold of ourselves and the world, rather than allowing awareness to spill over the margins to communicate intimately with the world in its nakedness. At some point we might notice that in the margins of our personal narrative there are a multitude of alternative perspectives on any situation. Knowing that our narrative is shaping life events, we could begin to break loose from its binding power and return our full attention to living in the world.

The subtlest aspect of the water principle misleads us away from our depths through its power to draw our attention to the vivid reflections reported by our senses. The problem is that we fail to see that it's our own awareness that is mirroring the world and giving form to what we're experiencing. Because our water element is the mind's natural capacity to reflect our surroundings, it seduces us to focus more on the reflection than on the *reflector*. Our attention automatically moves outward away from our invisible center toward the external world, but our awareness is itself the source of these reflections. Because many of us are externally focused, over time our own inner depths can begin to feel like an alien, an *other*, and become a source of fear.

From the perspective of the left-hand path, whatever happens in our life, painful or pleasurable, beautiful or grotesque, becomes a direct reflection of our immediate state of mind. The realization that we're actually inseparable from what we're observing creates a radical reversal in who we take ourselves to be. We begin to live in intimate relationship with the stream of life, no longer standing apart as an observer, but instead moving with the ebb and flow of events.

# 13

# The Water Element's Personal Touch

Because neurosis and sanity, samsara and nirvana, arise together, we're moved to both connect with and disconnect from the natural qualities of our inner elements. In the case of the water element, our personality or ego-self struggles to further its *own* survival by mimicking water's qualities, thereby distorting their expression.

When the wisdom aspect of water is dominant in our experience, we're highly observant and our perceptions can be crystal-clear and precise. We put a high premium on objective knowledge, and we're willing to sacrifice our own perspectives and opinions if we feel that it serves the truth. Our willingness to melt our rigid boundaries and flow with situations opens up unlimited perspectives, which can inspire original ways of seeing ordinary things. Like a moving stream of translucent water that reveals what's beneath its surface, when we embody the intelligence of the water element we're willing to risk vulnerability by openly sharing what lies beneath our surface. The water element's keen powers of observation inspire us to take delight in exploring the intricate details of things and to uncover our own blind spots, as we sense how we might develop our hidden potentials to function optimally.

The basic virtue of the water element is perception that's clear and precise, but it's also the intuitive vision that mirrors our interconnectedness with all things and beings. The circular physiology of the eye and its pupil, the circular shape of the sun, and the domelike quality of the open sky as it encompasses the curved horizon of the Earth, all suggest the theme of circularity that embraces everything within the visual field. Mirrorlike wisdom reflects this holistic image of life, where we can see ourselves as integral parts of the whole. Like being part of a team and working collaboratively with others to produce a finished product or service, we appreciate the efficacy of our interdependence.

In spite of our imperfections we may realize that we're a unique manifestation of being. The water element's quality of transparency is precisely what permits us to recognize our inseparability from Buddha nature itself, our deepest and most essential nature. We realize that we, ourselves, are not only a part of the totality of life, but a unique expression of it.

Our gift of mirrorlike wisdom can allow us to connect with big-picture thinking, as we realize that, moment by moment, our life and other people's lives are unfolding as they need to. The more contact and communication we have with our inner water, the more we experience life as coherent and meaningful, and we're able to communicate this clarity to others in ways that are understandable.

However, we can fall into the trap of feeling that we need to emotionally distance ourselves from experience in order to maintain objective observation. In this way we might disconnect from our own naturally existing water element. Our neurotic relationship with the water element rests on a core belief that by identifying with our inner witness we can protect ourselves from getting flooded by or submerged in powerful feelings. Our basic modus operandi is to establish order out of seeming chaos by creating a mental map of the world. Such an intellectual process can provide a brilliant synthesis, but it can also result in a tangle of information without true understanding.

Although we have the gift of lucid reflection, we can also imagine how things "should" optimally be. This idealistic tendency could lead to a misguided campaign to improve both ourselves and others, or to remedy situations in an attempt to make our world more symmetrical, exact, and perfect. We could misuse observation and analytic thinking as substitutes for real experience by living in the tower of mind in order to avoid feeling too much.

Fearful of getting overwhelmed by the influx of sensations and feelings, when our water element is expressed neurotically we're likely to feel that instinctual urges need to be suppressed, along with any sense of imperfection or personal failure. Such inconveniences break our stride on the way toward imagined perfection and our effort to tame disorder or chaos. Exerting rigid control over our desires and impulses often results in a loss of spontaneity and compromises our intimate connection with others, who can feel our bodily and emotional constriction. This effort to suppress our unruly feelings makes our interior world feel pressured and claustrophobic, which inevitably leads to irritation and anger. At that point, we're likely to become judgmental as we try to aggressively push the world away by intellectualizing our experiences so that we feel less vulnerable.

When we're under the influence of the water element, we're tempted to minimize our involvement in intimate relationships that we feel might drain us energetically. Wary of siphoning off too much of our life force, we instinctively move away from those whom we think have expectations of us, or we create firm boundaries to prevent ourselves from getting depleted by social demands.

In intimate relationships others may see us as too self-sufficient and not emotionally available. Even when we do show up, our partners often accuse us of lacking full involvement, as we tend to suppress our impulses and resist abandoning ourselves to spontaneous sensual play. Given our rigid standards for how others or situations "should" be, we can make our partners, family members, or friends feel self-conscious by our silent but palpable critical judgments and intolerance.

Preferring the safety of our intellect, we might experience interpersonal relationships as a burden, rather than a source of deep connection, pleasure, and enrichment. Although we have a unique gift for cognitive clarity and a deep sensitivity to beauty, our passion for precision and aesthetic refinement can become a substitute for truly loving another. We might replace intimate connection with family and friends with a thirst for elegant systems of thought or sublime beauty, which can lead to a growing disinterest in everyday life and an avoidance of the emotional work necessary to maintain friendships and intimate relationships.

# 14

# Everything We Meet Is Bright

We discover the essence of waterlike wisdom by interrupting the numbing effect of our continuous inner dialogue and our mechanical behaviors, both of which promote a sleeplike existence. The mirroring quality of the water element reflects the very powerful habitual patterns of thought and behavior that we've had for a whole lifetime, so that we see them for what they are—autonomous routines that run our life.

The spontaneous reflections of the water element may break through the cobwebs of our busy mind and provoke us to abruptly notice something about ourselves or our world with stunning clarity. Like being caught off-guard when we catch our reflection in a storefront window, we see our reflection objectively as others see us. The uncompromising quality of such a reflection, so direct and immediate, drops the scales from our eyes, suddenly revealing what has been hidden. This can be unsettling.

Water's mirrorlike wisdom is analogous to looking at our reflection in a mirror. When we walk away from the mirror, it's empty of our image. It reflects the moment beautifully, but it lets go of it instantly. Unlike a camera storing snapshots the way we humans store memories, a mirror doesn't retain past images. Imagine how a mirror would function if it weren't willing to let go of the innumerable images that it reflects. There would be millions of superimposed images of people, places, and situations from months and years of reflection.

In our usual state, we tend to look at our world through the frame of all of our yesterdays, through a kaleidoscope of superimposed memories. Here we can see the difference between reflection and projection, both aspects of the water element. When we're not mindful, we invariably project our collage of memories onto situations, superimposing our beliefs, prejudices, and expectations onto others. This process clutters our perceptual frame and plants seeds of potential complication because we're inserting our inventory of stuff into an otherwise neutral situation.

However, under the influence of water's wisdom aspect, when we release a thought, image, or memory and return to the quality of openness, we renew our readiness to objectively reflect who or what is simply there. As we practice letting go of the mind's contents, we discover that our experience shifts, or perhaps expands, deepens, or intensifies, revealing different facets and dimensions of both ourselves and our world. Unlike a snapshot that captures a moment in time, instead we open, relax, and yield to the waterlike flow of each succeeding moment. It could be the colorful parade of passersby as we sit at an outdoor café, or the buzz of crickets at dusk. An atmospheric crispness might suddenly draw out our senses into naked contact with the momentary form of this sight, this sound, this fragrance, this texture. We touch the moment with awareness and let go, again and again.

This practice can provoke irritation and anger because it deprives us of the comfort of our personal narrative and the predictability of our habits, leaving us exposed to uncertainty at how to go forward. The left-hand approach to the water element teaches us that anger, irritation, and defensiveness actually have the potential to sharpen our immediate presence because of their intensity and one-pointedness. When we relinquish our judgments about negative emotions and bring attention to their brute energy, they transform themselves into undistorted clarity, illuminating details we can now appreciate.

When we find ourselves reacting to our neighbor's playing of music, we might immediately become annoyed and irritated, as our attention narrows. Like a magnifying glass gathering the sun's rays into a penetrating point of light, our attention may clarify our attachment to silence and stillness, and our insistence that things be different than the way they are.

The practice of continually letting go invites the next moment to arise in a spontaneous and uncontrived way so that we can experience even a painful or grotesque situation with such penetrating clarity that it's transformed into something aesthetically gratifying, although not pleasurable. Our life gives us this precious moment, and the next, each emerging seemingly out of nowhere. The world asks only that we meet this living moment with warmth and curiosity.

Whereas our inner space element inspires us to open, pause, and be in our immediate experience, the clear awareness of the water element inspires us to find delight in personal discovery, as we experience either thought-provoking clarity or playfulness in the shape-shifting fluidity of the unfolding moment. Water's fluidity encourages us to bring a lightheartedness to changing circumstances. With an attitude of playful exploration, like a stream naturally flowing over rocks, we don't always need a fixed destination. We can appreciate the journey itself as the goal.

Randomly throughout the day, perhaps when brushing our teeth or stopping at a red light, we might flash on this sudden arising moment. We could simply open and allow the moment to reflect what's immediately there, cutting through the fuzziness of our inner dialogue. We might suddenly be thrust into the living moment by a gust of wind that slams a door shut. In the midst of an uneventful Sunday afternoon, perhaps our reverie of dreamlike thoughts is interrupted as we look out of our window to notice the emerald-green patina of the rolling hills in the distance. We might suddenly become aware of how the crackling of wood burning in our fireplace shatters the silence or how the aroma of French toast wafting from our neighbor's home seizes our attention, reminding us of everything wholesome and good.

Such moments return us to the *suchness* of life, where ordinary things reveal their magical, ineffable qualities. When we see ordinary events and situations with such clarity and precision, they appear brilliant and beautiful in their unpredictable rawness, inviting us to step into and savor the inexhaustible riches of our sensory world. In this way we return to the depth, meaning, and beauty of life, where we discover a sense of the extraordinary in ordinary events.

# 15

# What Buddha Might Recommend

Now take the opportunity to experience for yourself the wisdom energy of the water element.

## Water Element Meditation 1

Take a comfortably seated position for ten or fifteen minutes, keeping company with the natural cycles of your breathing as an aid to being present. Recognize that the stream of your thoughts doesn't have an ultimate destination, but is the natural play of the mind. Rest assured that while meditating there's no need to resolve any problem or conflict, or figure anything out.

Using your inner water element's power of reflection, notice the stream of your underlying thoughts and images as they're clearly reflected in your awareness. The moment you become aware of a thought or image, let go immediately and return your attention to being here, now.

The essence of the practice is to simply witness what's moving in the stream of your awareness and then immediately return your attention to your natural cycle of breathing or your physical presence.

## Water Element Meditation 2

Imagine that you've entered a primeval rainforest, perhaps something like the biblical Garden of Eden. In front of you there's a pristine waterfall gently descending into a shallow pool. The landscape surrounding the waterfall is lush with vegetation, embellished with tropical flowers and fruit trees, as pastel-colored birds chirp melodiously from their branches.

You feel completely safe and are drawn to take a seat beneath this waterfall. Much to your delight, you discover that the water is body temperature, and so pure that it's like liquid mist, spraying the surface of your head while also penetrating the pores of your scalp as it slowly enters the interior of your head, purifying everything it touches.

This pure water slowly wends its way from the top of your head down through your neck, spine, back, and chest, and the remainder of your torso as well as your arms and legs, making contact with all of your organs, tissues, glands, bones, and cells.

Practice visualizing this primeval water as a force of purification and healing, so that every part of your body it touches becomes bright, light, and cleansed. The essence of this meditation is to bring whatever thoughts and feelings arise into contact with the sacred water, so that any emotional complications are neutralized. After ten or fifteen minutes you can end the practice with the sacred water passing through the bottom of your feet, purifying your entire body and being.

## Practical Applications

Mirrorlike awareness refers to water's natural property of reflectiveness, which illuminates the things of our everyday world so that we see them clearly. Like a mirror our inner water element can objectively reflect, but in its distorted form we unconsciously project our thoughts and images onto situations, converting the world to a replica of ourselves. The repetitive use of language attributes common meanings to things and events, and completely shapes the way we perceive what we call reality. In this practice, we're trying to see through the transparency of words and language to glimpse what lies beyond them. The following are some domains where you can practice working with your inner water element.

### Choiceless awareness

When in the midst of an ordinary activity or situation, silently inquire, "What am I presently aware of?" or "Am I willing to be in touch with everything in my field of awareness?" Allow these questions to be catalysts for spontaneous awareness, without needing to figure anything out.

## Personal narrative

After a brief meditation session, sit in front of a mirror and gaze at yourself. This practice is more revealing if you're naked. While continuing to gaze at yourself, write out a truthful description of what you see in a matter-of-fact manner. Notice how your past associations, feelings, and judgments tend to shape what you're observing. Include them in your narrative by placing them in parentheses.

Next, continuing to sit in front of the mirror, describe what you're seeing, but instead of telling yourself the truth of what you're observing write the opposite of what you previously stated, describing qualities about yourself that you know are fabrications. Afterward, consider both descriptions as your idiosyncratic versions of yourself.

# Part Three

# Earth Element:
# Substance, Sensuality, and Stability

Like the autumnal harvest, our sense of embodiment and enriching presence permits us to luxuriate in the sensuality of taste, touch, and fragrance, as we feel our intimate connection with the community of all living beings.

**Qualities**
Equanimity, peacefulness
Sensuality
Patience
Fertility, generativity
Perseverance, fortitude
Gratitude

# 16

# If Earth Could Speak

I am the organic foundation of all life, the very substance of your body. I'm the opulence of your sensations and feelings, and the ferocity of your instincts. You're woven into the fabric of nature, and through your eyes and ears, your nose and mouth, and the sensations radiating through your body, I penetrate you and communicate my mysteries to you. Your inner earth reveals that there's a sympathetic relationship between you and the phenomenal world. If you're willing to reconnect with your body's natural sensuality, you'll discover that, like a luscious tropical jungle, your body is an erotic landscape.

Your capacity to feel into and relish experience with an unflinching eagerness reflects my virtue of equanimity. When you stay intimately connected to your inner earth, like a mountain that remains immovable and dignified whether it rains, snows, or is scorched by the sun's intense radiation, you'll remain solid, stable, and unshakable. Through your own inner earth I enable you to experience immovability and groundedness so that you can persevere through difficult experiences, until eventually there are no limitations to how deeply you can feel.

I'm the source of endless fertility, growth, and creativity in the bounty of the harvest. I bestow my magical quality of regeneration to all beings so that they can renew themselves after periods of lying fallow. I'm the mysterious energy that fertilizes the seeds of potentiality hidden within yourself.

However, if you disconnect from my earthy wisdom and power, you'll no longer be in sympathetic relationship with the natural world. You'll be plagued by the distorted perception of inner poverty, and feel distant from the eroticism of your own body. Instead of taking pleasure in being alive, you'll struggle to imitate my qualities of solidity, strength, and richness, but you won't find lasting gratification in any of your endeavors.

Yet, through your intimate connection with me, the unbridled electricity of your feelings will billow through your body and awaken your senses to the marvels of the phenomenal world. Stay close to me and you'll experience equanimity in the face of adversity, for difficult or painful seasons of life are followed by periods of renewed hope and growth. From the substance of your own inner earth, you'll cultivate confidence that the graceful cycles of nature and the seasons of your life have their own intelligence and unique rhythms. This is the way of Mother Earth.

# 17

# Our Body's Natural Eroticism

The left-hand path holds the view that all of life is sacred, and we're not merely creatures struggling to survive on a planet of shrinking resources. We don't have to embark upon a heroic quest to seek a transcendent realm, since nothing is lacking here on planet Earth. We have everything we need for our marvelous journey.

Earth is the organic foundation of life, the living organic being that we are. It's the very essence of our body, the richness and depth of our sensations and feelings—all of which are bridges between us and the external world. Earth is both organic embodiment and our body's embeddedness in the substance of our culture.

Earth represents the life substance we use to evolve toward our own fruition, symbolizing the harvest of our personhood, the very purpose of our human incarnation. Since everything that lives eventually dies, decomposes, and returns to the soil, the earth element holds the sum total of our past, yet its seeds contain the promise of what's yet to come. We're invited to give birth to what's truly unique within ourselves.

As we return to our senses and become more fully embodied, we spontaneously reconnect with our body's natural eroticism, in tune with our inner earth element. The beauty of our inherent earthiness lies in the discovery that our body is a diverse landscape of sensitivity. Rejoicing in the sensuality of everyday life affirms our most basic human wish: to take pleasure in simply being alive. The open secret is that embodiment can be a celebration of life.

The fragrant smell of wood burning in a fireplace, the distant sound of the surf, a cool summer breeze coming in from the

Pacific—all can open our senses and return us to the sensuality of our living body. Our inner earth element teaches us that through our eyes and ears, nose and mouth, and the sensations radiating through our skin-encapsulated body, the natural world penetrates and communicates its mysteries to us.

Our living body permits a silent conversation between us and the surrounding environment. The boundaries of our body are porous, more like membranes than barriers, permitting communication not only with the natural world and with others, but also with ourselves. Through somatic experience, we can enjoy the thrill of vivid sights, enchanting sounds, intoxicating fragrances, delectable tastes, and varied textures. Hearing the joyous sound of children playing or the roar of a motorcycle piercing the hum of traffic, feeling the sun benevolently bathing our face or hunger pangs stabbing our stomach—all can bring us back to what's most real in this moment: the sensuality of simply being alive.

We commonly feel that loneliness is caused by an absence of friends or a community of like-minded others, but perhaps we suffer alienation because we live at a distance from ourselves. If we're not intimate with our own body and its natural rhythms, we feel estranged from both ourselves and the natural world. Yet, when we walk out into a garden and give our undivided attention to the geometrically shaped succulents and the blossoming pink magnolias, our sense of community widens. We're joined to other species and find ourselves less alone.

Our body is also like an archaeological dig in that there are ancient layers of racial, cultural, familial, and personal adaptation that condition us to think and behave in predictable ways. Our parents' modeling of particular attitudes, emotional patterns, and characteristic behaviors, as well as their nonverbal prohibitions and taboos, are embedded in our flesh. At the same time, the body continually regenerates itself, creating new cells daily, so that in several months all the cells of our body are replaced by new ones. This generative quality of earth, embodied in the bounty of the harvest, is our own capacity for endless rebirth and creativity. In spite of the conditioning we received as children from our family and culture, when the urge to be our own person is stronger than the pull of the social collective, we step out on a new path in life.

Paradoxically, there's hope even in endings. When an aged sequoia falls to the forest floor, its life isn't completely over. Within a short span of time as it begins to disintegrate, lichens, mosses, and mushrooms make their home within its cadaverous trunk, as insects burrow through its bark to establish miniature societies. In death the sequoia offers immense hospitality to other beings who seek opportunities to further their own lives.

The earth reveals fertility and creativity where we least expect it. The devastating end of a relationship may signal the initiation into a fresh life with a remarkable new friend. By the end of our own life we may have contributed in unseen ways that enable others to thrive. None of us will ever know how deeply we've affected our community of friends and family, who carry us with them.

# 18

# Feminine and Masculine Aspects of Earth

The feminine aspect of the earth element includes the qualities of fertility, growth, and creativity, symbolized by the bounty of the harvest, but also our capacity to nurture and to be nurtured. We have the capacity to compassionately hold ourselves like a mother when we suffer and to respond to what we need without shame or embarrassment. Unless we're able and willing to give this to ourselves, we cannot hold others compassionately.

In the Buddhist mandala, the earth element is connected with the autumnal harvest, when Mother Nature comes to fruition, displaying her luscious abundance and continual generosity. When fruit is ripe, it automatically falls to the ground, and the earth element embodies this sense of selfless giving away. Autumn contains a poignant mixture of qualities. There's the richness and substance of the harvest, with its deep colors of yellow, gold, and saffron, but also a somber sense of death in the air, as autumn brings nature to the end of her annual cycle.

Yet, earth renews itself after periods of lying fallow. We all possess this magical feminine quality of regeneration. When we draw on the power of our inner earth, we don't lose heart even when we fail, we don't give up hope even when we meet with loss, and we don't remain stuck in despair even when we've lost someone precious. Our inner earth is inexhaustible in its capacity to give birth to new life. From the ashes of loss and failure we can rise like the mythological phoenix to begin something new.

Feminine earth is the capacity to feel into our experience, which provides us with an unshakable sense of presence. It's the simple and profound enjoyment of being wholly and completely here with our body, with our senses wide open. The virtue of our inner earth is equanimity—an unbiased approach to experience.

This capacity relishes experience with an eagerness that's indifferent to personal discomfort. Our inner substance allows us to appreciate the bitter and sweet qualities of life without being knocked off our center. We can marvel at the unbridled electricity of feelings as they sweep through our body in waves of energy, awakening our senses. Even unpleasant experiences have a surprising way of enriching our human journey.

It's like when we're angry at a friend because their words or actions feel like a betrayal; this may undermine our sense of safety and security but also help us to redefine the relationship and perhaps clarify the imperfection within all relationships.

While the feminine aspect of our inner earth embodies fertility and nurturance, the masculine aspect is our inherent capacity to be grounded and centered, unyielding and protective. Masculine earth is often symbolized by the majesty of mountains, which remain solid and unshakable, confident and commanding, whether they're battered by rain or snow, or assaulted by lightning and hailstorms. We can tap into our unswerving sturdiness to persevere through difficult or threatening experiences and not flinch under hardship. Learning to trust that every experience can fertilize the soil of our life, we stay open to the seeds of potential within our experiences. This is the meaning of equanimity.

Perhaps we were only able to partially understand some of our prior experiences. We might not have been mature enough to grasp the implications of such experiences, or we might have felt threatened or overwhelmed at the time and couldn't let them penetrate us fully. Many events have unfolded that have remained timelessly incomplete for us. Like seeds embedded in the soil of our body and mind, they still need to ripen so we can integrate them within our personality. Only with earth's feminine qualities of nurturance and gentleness and its masculine qualities of groundedness and solidity can we bring our seeds to maturity.

When we give ourselves permission to grieve a loss that we've been avoiding, it opens our heart and brings us into intimate contact with the source of our grief. By having the courage to allow ourselves to be vulnerable, we're penetrated to the core of our being. Something that was closed now opens up, permitting a renewed flow of energy and understanding. No amount of thinking takes us to the depths we experience when we relate with the living energy of our feelings and follow their currents.

Feelings of malaise, moodiness, and vague depression sometimes need to be overridden by the sacred indifference of masculine earth so that we can get on with our day. Yet, such amorphous feelings could suggest a connection between our present emotional state and something that we've either denied or haven't brought to completion. Our feminine earth principle may need to hold those ambiguous feelings with maternal solicitation until they find their voice and reveal their meaning to us.

The left-hand path encourages us to communicate with our emotions as energy, which is an entirely different experience than what most of us think of as having feelings. Our feelings are usually mixed with past associations and dramatic narratives, which add complication and confusion to the experience. We're often not sure of our relationship to our feelings, assuming that we either have to defend ourselves from their onslaught or act them out in order to get them off our chest.

Much like the earth itself, which supports all manner of flora and fauna, our inner earth's virtue of equanimity suggests that we cultivate an equal openness to the darker feelings of grief, remorse, and betrayal. The more we're willing to communicate with the depth and richness of these feelings, the more their energy provides guidance. Feelings of grief over loss are natural expressions of having a heart, of being human. There is an intelligence and a rhythm to our feelings that's particular to each one of us. Our feminine earth can open us to experience our feelings of sadness, loneliness, and abandonment, but masculine earth reminds us that we need not prolong and embellish our grief by telling ourselves the same tragic story. We also need to get on with our life. The greater our willingness to stay in direct contact with our body's inner movements and sensations, its rhythms and pulsations, the less likely we are to divide our world into the arbitrary categories of acceptable and unacceptable.

Responding from our heart and belly, and feeling deeply, opens us up to sensitive exploration. When we communicate directly with our feelings, permitting them to speak to us, they can reveal our real desires and hurts, until eventually we can accept and even love whoever or whatever was formerly unacceptable and unlovable.

The body is boundless, and each sensory experience can enrich us by taking us into the depth of life itself, where we're brought to the magical interface between ourselves and the world. Because all experiences are transient and passing, ultimately we're called to surrender them. Paradoxically, our willingness to let go transforms the passing caravans of ordinary experience into that which is precious and timeless.

When we're open to the passing images and sounds, tastes and fragrances, and feelings and moods, they move freely through us, unconstrained by our effort to make them fit within our scheme. With such equanimity the ordinary world reveals its exquisite suchness.

# 19

# The Seasons of Our Life

The left-hand path, like the perennial wisdom of many esoteric traditions, holds that human life is a microcosm of the macrocosmic universe. As above, so below. The Earth's goodness and beauty is found not only in the natural elegance of her rhythms, cycles, and seasons, but also in the seasons of our human life. The rhythms of both the natural world and our inner world unfold according to their own intelligence and timing. Viewed in this light, we don't have to struggle or manipulate our experiences as if we were always seeking a better deal.

There's the winter of inaction, where our projects may lie fallow—a time when we draw into ourselves for reflection, contemplation, and healing. Perhaps it's an uneventful time when nothing much seems to be happening in our life and we have more doubt than hope, more inertia than initiative, more melancholy than cheerfulness. Such a season invites us downward into our own depths, a place we wouldn't ordinarily go. Although such an experience may not be pleasant, there's often value in dropping down into the darker dimensions of our soul. By being willing to go there and experience our shadowy depths, we metabolize its destructive aspect, carving a place in our interior where such dark feelings can coexist on equal footing with our light and bright feelings.

Spring is when we experience periods of creativity, hope, or love, seemingly emerging out of the barren landscape of our psychological winter, as we find ourselves in movement with a renewed sense of energy. Unable to trace any singular cause for this delightful reversal, we simply take advantage of the resurgence of energy, sensing that now is the time to ride the currents of this season and launch ourselves full throttle into our life. Rather than becoming inflated or intoxicated with ourselves, we simply recognize that we're moving through a delightful cycle brought about by innumerable causes and conditions.

Summer may be a time when we're flourishing, as we find ourselves extended outward into the social network of our friends, family, and community. It could be a time of inspiration in love or creative work, as many pieces of our life come together to work synergistically in our favor.

And autumn is that time in our life when we reap the results of our efforts, as the seeds that we've been germinating reach fruition. Many factors beyond our individual efforts contributed to the maturation of our seeds, and so we're filled with gratitude and humility, knowing that such cycles don't last forever.

From the substance of our inner earth, we can cultivate confidence and conviction that the cycles of nature and the seasons of our life have their own natural intelligence, their own rhythms, and their own unique expressions. With inner earth as our foundation and the virtue of equanimity as our guide, we can embrace both beginnings and endings.

The inner season of winter returns again to offer possible respite and refreshment. Or perhaps this season invites us downward into our depths, where we pause to reflect, giving ourselves time and space to experience the ending of a phase of our relationship with our children or our partner, or perhaps the final stage of a project we've been working on for many months or years. Little by little we learn to allow all manner of experience to coexist—the good and the bad, the ugly and the beautiful—intuitively grasping that they emerge from and return to the same soil—our life.

Consequently, we can develop dignified composure when challenged by difficult circumstances, especially when enduring periods of loss and defeat. We remind ourselves that difficult or barren periods are often followed by periods of renewed hope, growth, and possibility.

# 20

# Imitation of Earth

When we're connected with the wisdom energy of earth, we appreciate the sumptuous offering of life without the acquisitive motive to possess the phenomenal world. With inner earth as our foundation we can allow all kinds of experiences to coexist without being swayed by challenging circumstances or seduced by enticing invitations. This quality is the virtue of equanimity.

Yet, some of us have a peculiar sensitivity that exaggerates the massive and awesome quality of life. We tend to feel dwarfed by comparisons with the substance of other people's lives, or with the lives of celebrities we see on TV. We may become haunted by the fear of losing our ground, our center of command, our power spot in life. Ironically, when we're connected with our natural, uncontrived earth element, we *are* the ground of being— the source of natural wealth and the abundance of possibility.

The problem begins once we fall out of alignment with our inner earth and feel compelled to possess its vitality and power. Once captured, earth loses its natural, living quality. It's easy to see how this could happen. Life seems to require so much of us. There seems to be one compelling thing to do after another, seemingly without respite: the dentist appointment for our root canal, the need to replace the taillight on our car, or attending to our sick teenager. The unavoidably repetitious situations, the irritating people who regularly press our buttons, the uncompromising urgency to pay our bills on time, and the expectations from significant others—all can feel like too much. We might not feel up to the challenge of meeting the world head-on.

When the demands of life seem overwhelming and we feel that who we are isn't enough—that we're not as smart, skillful, successful, or potent as we ought to be—the relationship with our inner earth element has become neurotic. At such times of self-doubt, we tend to dissociate from our inner earth and create an unintended psychological abyss. Losing our connection with our own roots we're left feeling deprived and abandoned, estranged from the source of our inner richness.

This inner division begins with the denial of our feelings of vulnerability and powerlessness, of not being enough or not having enough. The distorted perception of inner poverty is precisely what causes us to feel dwarfed by the monumental quality of life or the seeming bigness of others.

As we fall out of alignment with our inner earth, we cut ourselves off from the instinctual wisdom that embraces the natural goodness of life itself. In a misguided effort to feel more real, we fall prey to a poverty mentality that paradoxically triggers the reflex to inflate ourselves. Perhaps we use all of our credentials and possessions trying to imitate earth's natural abundance, its qualities of richness, solidity, and expansiveness. In this way we give birth to false or neurotic earth.

Driven by feelings of inner emptiness we can't seem to get enough food, sex, companionship, or stimulation to fill ourselves up. Unlike the unconditional richness of earth, our imitation of the earth element is contaminated with excessive desiring, an undiscriminating hunger for intense experience. We're caught in the neurotic pursuit of substitute pleasures to compensate for feeling insufficient.

Our insatiable desire for more stimulation prevents lasting intimacy with either ourselves or another, because the intensity of our yearning outshines any experience of possible fulfillment. We might recruit others to give us the love, affection, and approval that we're unable to give to ourselves, wanting more from them than they can possibly give. Cultivating a completely secure and proud way of looking at ourselves, we try to dispel our feelings of insubstantiality and insignificance by incorporating others into our territory.

We're often unaware of the sadness and grief we carry because of our estrangement from our own essential earth qualities. No matter whom we're with or what we're doing, we seem to be searching for a lost connection with our own depths. We want to return to that unmistakable sense of home, the experience of profound belonging and of homecoming. In a misguided way we try to establish such a foundation by making personal territory out of our experiences, hoping to smooth over the feeling of standing out as an individual amidst other beings and things of seemingly greater substance and magnitude than ourselves.

The irritating edge of duality of self and other creates constant sparks of energy. The sparks can be provocative, energizing, and invigorating, but they can also cause discomfort and fear. On the left-hand path, tuning into this energy gives us a unique opportunity to take advantage of any state of mind or experience by riding the energy of situations rather than having them ride us.

When we relate with the basic substances of our emotions, we discover that we're in touch with energy—the neutral vitality, power, and force of life itself. We don't regard any part of ourselves as alien, but can instead use whatever life offers us. We learn to ride our emotions as if riding a succession of waves. In this way we never have to fear losing our ground.

The good news is that the very sense of disconnection from our earth element can spark a reconnection with what's original within us. In this unbiased approach to life, both positive and negative experiences can coexist without triggering the reflex to grasp what's pleasurable or reject what's painful. Tapping into our own earth element we can feel gratitude for the richness of every situation.

Through appreciation of our bodily sensations and feelings, the earth element reassures us that we're connected to our immediate environment and to one another. We're reminded that our body and our sensory organs are the portals through which the natural world communicates with us and makes love to us. There's always some form of generosity and abundance implicit in our experiences. Embodiment returns us to the simple joy of being alive.

# 21

# Earth's Shadow

We might feel that in the privacy of our own mind there's no harm in allowing random thoughts to play out, or in entertaining various inner narratives, since such activities are invisible and don't really impact others. This casual relationship with ourselves overlooks the reality that our mind is like fertile soil. The shadow side of earth is that it doesn't distinguish between positive and negative seeds, but nurtures both. Earth's virtue of equanimity invites opposite qualities to find a place in its garden.

Our psyche or deep mind is continually active, energetically nourishing whatever seeds we've planted in its domain. These subconscious seeds are the content of our life—our hopes and fears, the people and situations we value and cherish, and the things that we fear and loathe. The implications of this principle aren't trivial. We usually don't take stock of the seeds we're planting in the fertile soil of our mind, but all of our experiences leave energetic traces or impressions. The accumulation of these seeds predisposes us to think and behave in characteristic ways, and forms the basis of our personality.

A frequently repeated thought, image, or behavioral sequence creates neurological and somatic pathways. We can be drawn to preexisting avenues that lead both to desired outcomes as well as to dead-end destinations we didn't consciously choose. If we don't exercise mindfulness, we inadvertently develop patterns of thought, attitude, speech, and behavior that, like irresistible forces of nature, shape our personality and the contours of our life.

Our deep mind, like the material soil of the earth element, is the magical crucible that stores, germinates, and brings *thought-*

*seeds* to fruition. Although each seed is a product of the past, it naturally seeks to complete itself in the future when conditions are ripe. Years ago there was a story in the news about a group of archaeologists who, upon opening a four-thousand-year-old Egyptian sarcophagus, discovered a bowl of seeds among other artifacts meant to provide resources in the afterlife for the mummified pharaoh. Out of curiosity one of the archaeologists planted some of the seeds to see whether, after four millennia, a unique species of plant would still be able to grow. Remarkably, the seeds did grow after four thousand years of dormancy.

The seeds in our mind can lie dormant for a very long time. They merit our attention and skillful handling because thoughts aren't innocent. They don't lie inert like nickels and dimes under the living-room carpet, but are psychoactive packets of potentiality, both positive and negative. When external circumstances come together in particular ways, they can trigger specific thought-seeds to mushroom instantly, along with behaviors that may not feel either intentional or rational.

These subconscious seeds might be the unresolved and uncooked kernels of prior experiences, the conflicts we're struggling with, or our dormant hopes and fears. They aren't static entities; they can spring from potentiality to actuality in a flash. If we've been in the habit of disapproving of ourselves and stewing in feelings of being devalued by others, during a holiday visit back home one slip of our father's tongue or his quizzically raised eyebrow could throw us into a rage despite our good intentions.

On the other hand, our virtuous seeds incline us to love the truth, strive toward authenticity, and try to make the world a better place than we found it. Our reaffirmation of gratitude and our practice of forgiveness incline us to speak from the heart, so that when we're confronted by a hostile individual we might be able to take the wind of aggression out of their sails through nonviolent communication.

The progression of thought to word and then to behavior implies that much of our experience is mindlessly automatic, occurring beneath the radar of awareness. Buddhism has historically used the image of a seed to explain the notion of *karma*, the law of cause and effect, action and reaction.

The underlying motive behind the karmic force is the blind compulsion to reinforce our idea of ourselves, who we imagine ourselves to be. The birth of ego is simultaneous with the birth of our shadow, everything about ourselves that we're struggling *not* to be. The way that we preserve our manufactured sense of self is by identifying with what's ego-reinforcing, rejecting what's threatening, and ignoring what's neutral or ambiguous because it doesn't provide enough feedback for our fabricated sense of self. The point is that we're continually manipulating our experiences to reinforce the *me* in almost all of our activities.

According to Buddhist tradition, first we have to tame our mind before we train it. Initially, when we practice equanimity our tangential thoughts and conflicting emotions are allowed to arise, but they're experienced as having *one taste*. In other words, when we treat our thoughts and feelings as more or less equivalent, they don't get nourished by our obsessive attention, nor do they get buried in our psyche as catalysts for future automatic behavior. Because we're neither denying nor overevaluating them energetically, they slowly begin to lose their electrical charge, and are less able to shape our behaviors.

Twenty-six hundred years ago the Buddha instructed us how to walk the path of liberation by watching our thoughts with care and by encouraging them to spring from love, born out of concern for all beings. When we hold a compassionate frame of mind, we transform our seeds—our thoughts, feelings, memories, and impulses—so that they take on an enlarged meaning and value.

Although every seed seeks individual expression, nature's intention is to grow its seeds in cooperation, harmony, and balance within the whole ecological system. In the human domain, when we hold a compassionate perspective, our seeds are reframed out of empathy for all beings, aligning themselves with Mother Nature's big picture. This cultivates our seeds to grow in harmony with the community of both human and nonhuman life.

By shifting our focus of attention away from our manufactured sense of self, we train ourselves to see others as no less important than ourselves. We can honor ourselves without reinforcing our ego, and protect the integrity of our being with effective boundaries, without negatively judging others with whom we disagree. No longer ignoring life's ambiguity, we can learn to live with uncertainty.

# 22

# The Earth Element's Personal Touch

As planet Earth redistributes solar and terrestrial energies equally to nourish all of life upon and within it, when our earth element is dominant in our experience, we can be protective, nurturing, and generous. Like a mother caring for her young, we're staunch advocates for those in need; we're emotionally supportive, and have the potential to connect deeply with others. Like earth's impartial nurturance of all seeds, we have an innate capacity to nurture all states of mind, finding value and uniqueness in all experiences. We can gratefully accept what life offers us without judgment, and can remain undisturbed when confronted by challenging circumstances.

Feeling the support of our inner earth, we develop steadfastness and balance to persist as experiences unfold, without the need to force anything. Having sensitivity to both the beauty and the pain of life, we're able to communicate subtle truths about the human condition, and to offer others both deep understanding and emotional nurturing. No longer acting on the assumption of inner deficiency, we embody the abundant richness and vital energy of the natural world.

Realizing that we're already unique expressions of nature's substance, we don't feel the need to inflate ourselves with pride or false earth. Embodying the virtue of equanimity, we're centered in ourselves, rooted in our own depths, no longer needing to stand out from others as being special. Willing to experience our own vulnerability and our need for love, we're able to cut through the reflex of always needing to be strong and domineering. Like the unapologetic abundance of the harvest, we can be self-revealing, emotionally honest, and highly empathic.

However, when we lose our connection with our inner earth,

we inadvertently cut ourselves off from the instinctual wisdom that appreciates the natural goodness and vitality of life. We compensate for this disconnection by trying to mimic these qualities, but we're rarely convinced of our real substance or worth, and continue to feel driven by feelings of inner emptiness. Unlike the unconditional richness of earth, which provides the reassurance of firmness beneath our feet, our imitation of the earth element involves excessive effort and striving.

In the neurotic expression of earth the core belief is that we're either not enough or don't have enough. No longer intimate with the sensory world of fragrances, textures, and tastes—like the late-afternoon light pouring through our window or the distant murmuring of a brook—a feeling of deprivation and inadequacy lingers beneath the radar of our awareness and stimulates our hunger for more stimulation and for more personal expression. Ironically this false sense of deficiency is self-validating as we take on limitation but get satisfaction from it. Trying to avoid the feeling of inner deficiency through displays of generosity and demonstrations of our richness, we hope to reestablish a link with our inherent solidity and depth. This strategy aims to restore the feeling of being whole and complete again, but in a self-centered way. We may believe that we shouldn't have feelings of neediness, powerlessness, and vulnerability, but these very feelings are precisely what we need to integrate within our personality in order to be whole.

Our undiscriminating hunger for intensity is an effort to replicate the monumental quality of earth. Feeling alienated from our natural earthy state we seek emotional intensity as a way of making ourselves feel grounded and authentic. There are many ironies in the effort to reconnect with our earth element once we've disconnected from it. Sensing an inner hollowness, our need to monopolize other people's attention is insatiable. We're repeatedly drawn to intense sexual-romantic relationships, but the heightened sensations only temporarily fill our void and leave us hungry for more stimulation. We often minimize the very feelings of pleasure we so desperately seek, because to permit ourselves to be gratified puts us in the exposed position of acknowledging our need for others.

At some point we might recognize that the denial of our soft feelings of vulnerability and dependence has sabotaged genuine communication and intimacy in all of our relationships. Minimizing the value of sensitivity, tenderness, and our own limitations has caused us to be unknowingly insensitive to others. The painful sense of disconnection from our earth element can lead to a genuine yearning for reconnection with what's original and unconditioned within us. Our need to be authentic could inspire the courage to drop into the deepest aspects of ourselves to connect with our inner richness. The realization that our sense of inner poverty has stemmed from separation from our own substance begins the process of realignment with the wisdom energy of our inner earth.

# 23

# Practicing Equanimity

Because of the dominance of our internal dialogue when neurotic earth predominates, we may be shocked to discover that we're largely disembodied, living in the abstract realm of our inner conversations, and not in sympathetic relationship with either our body or the natural world.

To connect with the wisdom of earth we have to become sensitive to both our inner landscape of changing moods, feelings, and impulses, as well as to the outer landscape of shifting forms and energies. The path leading to embodiment involves appreciation of the natural eroticism of eating, bathing, walking, breathing, and enjoying intimate friendship as well as the sound of the cawing crows perched above us. Like earth's springtime, the promise or hint of what's to come draws us out from our interior into the visible and tangible world of color and form, which simultaneously finds a place within our interior.

When we truly inhabit our body and open our senses to life, small things stir something in us, and transport us once again to an enchanted world. Like lovers, we might find ourselves naturally savoring *these* delicious tomatoes in olive oil and basil, or delighting in the sensual feel of *this* silk scarf, or thrilling at the scintillating sensation of plunging into *this* mountain lake. What if we experienced mountains, streams, and forests, as well as old clocks, favored armchairs, and neighborhood grocery stores as having their own unique life? By sensing the soulfulness of such things, we breathe life into them, and as a result they come closer to us.

Yet, there's something perplexing about the practice of appreciating the body's natural eroticism. Although somatic experiences can be enriching, they're all transient. Because of the impermanent nature of all phenomena and the evanescent nature of all experience—sacred and profane—we ultimately come to surrender all experiences. By encouraging ourselves to connect with our inner earth, we may recall that during autumn grapes drop from the vine and apples fall effortlessly from trees. The earth principle within us gives us the courage and the capacity to let go and let be.

Further obstacles that aren't so obvious need to be overcome before we can embrace the majesty of earth. By the time we become adults, we carry a huge amount of body armor because we've internalized so many injunctions, so many "Thou shalt nots" under the dominance of our inner parent. As children the superego initially started out as our surrogate parent and protector, but then began to stalk the free-spirited child within us for being a little too spontaneous and freewheeling. Whenever we transgressed the boundaries of our parental and societal admonitions, our superego punished us with feelings of guilt, remorse, and anxiety, sabotaging possibilities for exploration, understanding, and enjoyment.

The practice of equanimity, or *one taste*, is the left-hand antidote to the disproportionate number of warnings, cautions, and disapprovals we've received. This expansive attitude undermines the critical inner parent, the source of our negative judgments. This practice also undermines the ego or self-created image we hold of ourselves, because ego can only survive where there's comparison and conflict. In the absence of the categorical opposites of self or not-self, friend or enemy, right or wrong, the ego is unable to define and distinguish itself. The ego needs to have an adversary or the sense of otherness to know what it is, by virtue of what it is *not*. When we practice earth's virtue of equanimity, we're equally open to all situations and all states of mind as *one taste*, in that they reveal the multiplicity of faces of life's unified tapestry. The impartiality of earth doesn't mean that all experiences high and low, sacred and profane, *feel* the same, or that we can no longer differentiate one feeling from another. Equanimity is the equal openness to communicate with all manner of diverse experiences. When our approach to experiences is unbiased, there are no longer limitations to how deeply we can feel, or how expansive our experiences can be. Equanimity is the difficult practice of aligning ourselves with situations as they are, not as we wish them to be. We might stumble upon hurt feelings of failure or cowardice, owing to a time when we lacked the courage to do the right thing. We may have carried this wound for decades, perhaps rationalizing our feelings around our shortcoming. Or perhaps we've beaten ourselves up with shame or blame, feeling that we haven't earned the right to be happy. Or we might be defending ourselves by denying our feelings altogether. In either case there's no real movement forward. Equanimity by contrast makes naked contact with our wound without blame or justification, relating with it as energy. We learn to feel into it, touching it but also letting it go so that our wound doesn't become a solid fixture within us.

Lastly, we might continue to stay in contact with the energy of the wound but as if looking or feeling with a wide-angle lens. This gives us a sense of context so that we intuit how it got to be this way, what function our suffering serves, and how it protects us from seeing something about ourselves that we've judged as inferior. We might also remember the pain and confusion we were in at the time.

The challenge of the left-hand path is seeing that our resistance toward accepting what is, and our attachment to the way things "should" be, is based on our unresolved grievances and conflicts. The practice of acceptance, gratitude, and forgiveness is how we embody equanimity. The left-hand path reminds us of the importance of expressing gratitude for the daily blessings of our human life, great and small. Contemplating our good fortune in having a human body and mind, we gratefully appreciate the wonders of sight, sound, smell, taste, and feeling, and our human awareness, which allows us to know the world. We give thanks for the enriching quality of our intimate relationships, our capacity to love another, and the network of family and friends who love and appreciate us.

Forgiveness is more complicated and subtle. We practice forgiving ourselves for being less than perfect, forgiving the world for not being like a supportive and nurturing parent, and eventually forgiving others for mindlessly hurting us. Sometimes others are guilty of having committed behaviors that caused us harm, either intentionally or unintentionally. We neither excuse nor forget their behavior, but we can let go of our clenched fist of resentment.

Through forgiveness we can open the interpersonal space between ourselves and those who have hurt us so that more possibilities exist for communication and connection. We might recognize how painful it is to put others outside of our heart. To the extent that we've exiled people to a dark, lonely place where we have withheld love or positive attention, we've transformed ourselves into jailers.

Forgiveness is counterintuitive because we may feel that it's natural to be angry or resentful toward those who have harmed us. But once we forgive them, we've taken down the barrier of emotional barbed wire and electricity, of separation and negative judgment, and have now opened up possibilities that didn't exist before.

Conversely, we may have caused others pain in the past, which could be another formidable wall exiling ourselves from potential relationship and community. By recognizing the pain we were feeling at the time, we come to understand how we may have committed actions that were insensitive, mean-spirited, cowardly, or just plain childish. Although we may be attached to the idea that we deserve to suffer, the key is to remember the pain and confusion we were in when we committed these particular actions. We meet our embarrassment and shame with compassion and forgiveness.

Equanimity marks the transition from resistance to acceptance, from no to yes. It doesn't mean we give ourselves permission to act out any impulse that pops into our head or seizes our hormones. Instead, it encourages us to recognize that as soon as we put up a wall to defend ourselves from what appears to be unpleasant or threatening, we've made an adversary out of an unwanted state of mind or a person or situation. This resistance is a denial of what life is presenting to us at this moment.

When we say yes to situations as they're unfolding, we stop demanding that external things make us happy or safe. When we relax our demands that the world be other than the way it is, everything becomes more peaceful. Beyond our personal narrative about life, equanimity opens us up to the whole of life, both the bitter and sweet. Equanimity doesn't fear the dark or strange side of life, and isn't attached to perfection or absolute truth. The left-hand path points to what lies beyond society's conventional boundaries, which may lead to unknown places within ourselves that can both enlarge and enrich our world.

Earth's virtue of equanimity is the experience of being rooted in our own depths, connected with the source of being itself. It's the wisdom that sees the value in all things and in all states of mind, even in those areas within ourselves that remain unresolved. Our acceptance of the truth of where we are, the truth of what we're experiencing, and the truth of who we are, takes us to a deeper place beyond ego's judgments of good and bad.

By daring to be open we might discover novel perspectives and more complex forms of relationship with others, both human and nonhuman, where perhaps we can forgive what seemed unforgivable. Yet, not every question has an answer, and not all of our problems and conflicts can be resolved. Equanimity also means that we let some things remain incomplete for the time being and move on with our life, knowing that we may come back to this place at a later date.

# 24

# What Buddha Might Recommend

Again, direct experience can enable you to embody the teachings, so take the time for the meditations and practices in this chapter.

## Earth Element Meditation

Take a comfortable seated position, and give yourself ten to fifteen minutes. Bring your full attention to your body. Feel yourself physically present, and relax into the simple pleasure of being without struggle or complication. When you experience feelings, distressing or delightful, immediately drop the narrative and any judgments associated with those feelings, and bring your attention to their energy, not the story connected to them.

As long as the feelings are prominent, continue to relate with their energy, and notice whether they expand or contract, intensify or become soft and diffuse. When these feelings become somewhat neutral or bland, return your attention to your sense of physical presence and the rhythmic cycles of your breath. If other strong feelings arise, repeat the process of communicating with their energy.

The earth principle embodies groundedness, solidity, steadfastness, and an unbiased approach toward all experience. Like a mountain, which remains steady, undisturbed, and dignified whether it's scorching hot or frigid cold, you also remain steady in the midst of your feelings. By refraining from making judgments and evaluations, all your feelings share a common ground as the play of earth's energies, having equal legitimacy.

## Practical Applications

The earth element provides the physical substance out of which we shape our life. As the earth is endlessly creative, we can draw on our inner earth to harvest and transform our unique qualities into creative expressions. The following are some domains where we can practice working with the earth element.

### Sensations, feelings, and moods

At any moment of the day, abruptly bring your attention to your entire body and momentarily relax into a sense of bodily presence for as long as you can. Enjoy the sensual pleasure of being anchored in your body without an ongoing narrative. Try to be with the quality of your somatic experience as it unfolds, without making up a story about what's going on. Move with the energetic flow of being embodied.

Initially, if you're unable to know what you're feeling, stay with the sense of your body a little while longer until you can discern physical sensations, such as hot or cold, lightness or heaviness, tightness or looseness. These are usually the precursors to actual feelings, such as joy or sadness, anger or love. There's nothing that you have to do about what you're feeling. Simply experience it.

Inquire whether you're aware of what you're feeling. Is your relationship to your feelings one of acceptance, appreciation, and inquisitiveness, or do you experience confusion, fear, or defensiveness? Do you get a sense of which moods are more characteristic for you than others? There are no right or wrong answers to these questions. They are intended to deepen your somatic sensitivity.

### Nature

Feeling your body as an expression of nature can open up your connection with and appreciation of Mother Earth. We all take part in her natural rhythms and cycles, and the wisdom of her elements. Our interdependence with the natural world encourages us to engage in loving relationships with our own body, with animals and plants, and with favorite geographical areas that feel like power spots.

Inquire whether you feel a connection with the earthy aspect of your own body, with its natural rhythms and cycles, with the wisdom of your feelings. If you're unable to appreciate the power and beauty of either your body or the natural world, rather than negatively judge this as a deficiency, give yourself permission to be with your experience exactly as it is. Try to be patient if understanding or appreciation doesn't arrive when you expect.

### Ancestry

We're part of nature and share in innumerable networks that provide sustenance for us and others. Contemplate your relationship with your extended family, and with your ethnic, racial, genetic, and cultural roots. Consider the transmission that you have received from these networks and what contribution they've made to your life.

Inquire whether you can truly separate and distinguish yourself from these networks of relationships.

# Part Four

# Fire Element:
# The Heat of Passion and the Light of Illumination

The radiant and magnetic energy of the fire element draws us to intimate relationships, inflames us with love and sexuality, opens our heart with the warmth of compassion, and illuminates what's murky and unclear, differentiating neurosis from sanity.

**Qualities**
Love, compassion
Passion, desire
Creativity
Enthusiasm, joy
Vulnerability
Beauty

# 25

# If Fire Could Speak

I am primordial desire, the magnetic power of attraction, the wish to be loved and to be loving. I'm the driving force of your passion, the pulsation of pleasure, and your primal urge to merge with whomever or whatever is desirable. I'm the spontaneous combustion of your brilliance and joy, and your charisma to infuse relationships with aliveness. I'm all manner of self-expression and creativity, and every nuance of delight and enjoyment.

My fire is the magnetism that draws desirable others to you, as you're irresistibly drawn toward them. I dissolve your boundaries, suspend your inhibitions, and seduce you into merging with your beloved to rejoice in their happiness and empathize with their suffering. I'm the binding quality of love and compassion, and communication and communion.

I'm the light of your inner vision, which clarifies details that are indistinct and confusing so you can distinguish one thing from another, discerning truth from falsehood, and neurosis from sanity. Using the brilliant flames of your inner fire you can clarify your many aspects in order to establish intimacy with yourself and distinguish healthy from neurotic forms of desire.

Be warned that if your inner fire gets colonized by your ego, you'll use desire in distorted ways to fill your illusory sense of inner hollowness. You'll be tempted to draw others to yourself and use them as kindling to ignite your dwindling enthusiasm and joy, keeping you bound to the wheel of repetition and dissatisfaction.

However, as you dare to awaken your heart, allowing fire energy to burn bright, you'll relate to the world with tenderness and deep appreciation for life itself, with all of its ambiguity, conflict, and complexity.

# 26

# The Exuberant Heart of Fire

The fire element is about magnetism—drawing desirable others to us—as we're irresistibly drawn toward them. Fire is associated with spring, the most alluring and captivating phase of nature's cycle. This is the season of rebirth and rejuvenation, a time when buds suddenly appear on branches and green shoots break the earth's surface with promise. Through its colorful and vivid display, spring sets the stage for the frenzy of mating, when all species are drawn to their gender opposites to enact the timeless ritual of sexual embrace. There's hopefulness and positive expectation in the air.

Our own inner fire heightens our sensitivity to beauty and is the source of passion and pleasure, desire and seduction, and the urge to merge. Without the fire of desire there would be no contact, communication, or bonding between entities. Nothing in the natural world would ever happen, for without the heat of attraction we wouldn't relate to one another intimately, let alone mate. Fire's combustibility inflames our passions beyond reason, ignites our enthusiasm, and sparks sudden creative surges.

Eros, the mythological Greek god of love and sexuality, brought the cosmos into existence through primordial desire. Eros is the magnetic power to attract and to be attracted, the natural desire to be loved and to be loving, to engage in romantic relationships, sensual pleasure, and aesthetic experience. When we feel desire or sexual attraction for another, there's electricity in the air as we suspend inhibition, cross boundaries, and seek intimacy with our idealized beloved.

Fire as eros is the primal desire to extend ourselves into our surroundings or to draw others toward us, as we yearn for fusion with whoever or whatever is desirable. This hunger for our world draws it close to us, allowing us to feel at home. The warm smile of recognition from an Arab grocer, the old homeless woman who says "God bless you" when we tip her tin can, the sensuous texture of the bark of an ancient sequoia, or an early-morning kiss from our loved one—all of these reassure us that we belong to this marvelous world, and it to us.

Because of our tenderhearted willingness to love our world, we incarnate the visible, audible, and palpable forms of the natural world through our eyes, ears, nose, mouth, and body. Enjoying the brilliant cumulus clouds floating across the deep-blue sky, the sound of children playing in a pile of leaves, a sudden spring shower that ignites a frenzy of movement, holding the hand of an ill parent, or delighting in the fragrance of freshly mowed grass, the natural world arises within and comes to life through us. Desire alchemically transforms the beings and things of everyday life into living presences who now live within us. By cherishing the tangible forms of everyday life, we restore soul to the world.

On the left-hand path, this intimate connection with life is called *sacred view*. The ordinary world has always been sacred, radiating a living energy that animates all things and beings. Primordial desire, as opposed to neurotic desire that wants to possess, is the catalyst that opens us to love. The fire element within us is the value of relatedness and relationship—the magnetizing energy that draws desired qualities toward ourselves, ranging from loyal friendships to sexual fusion, from artistic and aesthetic experience to spiritual union. However, before we can find lasting value in our relationships with others and experience intimacy with our everyday life, we first need to love ourselves with the warmth of our own fire. This self-love may be our most daunting challenge.

Our capacity to have compassion for others depends on our ability to be vulnerable and in touch with our own pain. This openness may mean having the courage to listen to the wounded child within us, the stunted emotional patterns of our youth, or our bitter disappointment for the life we didn't live. The fire element teaches us to honor the individuality of every part of ourselves, both the small and the great, the light and the dark. Reclaiming each part as an essential element of the whole tapestry brings our forgotten parts into a larger sense of self.

Being whole means communicating with and eventually loving these diverse aspects of ourselves. Our inner fire element is the magnetic force that draws our many aspects into complex and elegant configurations, giving birth to the truly unique individual that we are.

# 27

# Feminine and Masculine Aspects of Fire

At the horizon, the soft pastel-red color of the setting sun signals a time of repose, a drawing inward of our attention and energy after our day's labors are done, a time when we can relax, contemplate, and meditate. In this context, fire is associated with crossing a threshold into the world of meditative vision and intuition. The feminine warmth of empathy melts the boundary between conscious and nonordinary states of mind, lending value and significance to our daily experiences, while the masculine light of inner vision illuminates what's invisible to our daylight consciousness.

The feminine aspect of the fire element is the energy of warmth and compassion and the binding quality of love and empathy. Motivated by the desire to communicate and to commune, the fire of compassion dissolves the boundaries between ourselves and others, as we draw them closer to ourselves or we're drawn closer to them, joining us with our world. We can appreciate the immediate presence of another on their own merits as we sense the inestimable value of every individual we meet.

The feminine wisdom energy of fire melts the artificial boundaries between the social image we present to the world and our shadow or hidden self, bringing together what we've formally rejected or denied into a state of wholeness. Fire's fearless love is the courage to allow contradictory opposites to coexist within our own personality.

Fire's masculine virtue is the awareness that distinguishes samsara from nirvana, the neurotic aspect of our relationship with money, food, and sex from their sane and healthy expressions. Fire's heat burns the fabric of our chattering monkey mind and illuminates the aspects of ourselves that are more primary and profound. The masculine energy of fire illuminates and clarifies details that would otherwise remain indistinct and imprecise. Whereas the water element enables us to distinguish our subjective version of things from what's objectively there, our inner fire can clarify the different dimensions of ourselves and our experiences.

Perhaps there's a part of us that's obsessed with survival, or another that urgently needs to feel connection with community. Although we may be overly ambitious, yet another dimension within us is self-sacrificing and compassionate. While our rebellious spirit seeks independence from all outer influence, at the same time, we could be terrified to step out of our box and risk failure and isolation.

Masculine fire recognizes that these many facets exist within us, so that we don't have to become confused about who we are. When we honor each of our parts and embrace them with love and compassion — the feminine qualities of fire — they allow us to be transparent to ourselves, offering insight into the complexity of our personality.

With the masculine light of awareness and the feminine warmth of compassion, we can hold the tension between surface and depth, between the patterns of our personality and the unfathomable depth of our soul, between the surface play of daily events and the profound mystery underlying their manifestation.

As we bring the male and female aspects of the fire element into balance within ourselves, we initiate a sacred marriage. The feminine fire of compassion magnetizes the unacceptable parts of ourselves and the parts of the world that we've rejected, and binds together what's divided within us. The masculine aspect illuminates and clarifies these many dimensions of our experiences, lending meaning, value, and significance to them. No matter where or in what condition we find ourselves, even in sickness and despair, awareness and love are there, burning bright.

Consider our possible disappointment with ourselves because of a series of projects and plans that still remain incomplete, or our lack of courage to meet the challenges of our marriage, which requires ever-changing adaptation; perhaps these can be revisioned as the warp and woof of life's rich tapestry. Our step-by-step walking makes the road that is our life. The journey *is* the goal. When we free ourselves from the neurotic tendency to grasp or reject particular experiences, we begin to realize how our nonbiased appreciation of the little details of daily life sparks our journey forward. The union or sacred marriage of masculine and feminine energies gives birth to the awakened heart, a ruthless love that doesn't ostracize those who appear to be different or exclude what feels alien. We remain open and willing to communicate with whom or what our life presents to us, valuing others in their unique humanness, allowing them to be as they are, and not extensions of ourselves.

When we integrate the masculine quality of discernment and the feminine qualities of warmth and compassion, we're enacting on an individual level the larger creative process where new forms of relationship and new life come into being. This courageous love of the awakened heart allows us to relate to the world with tenderness and with a deeper appreciation for life itself in all of its complexity and conflict.

# 28

# Distortions of Eros

There are two fundamentally different kinds of desire: One is a natural expression of love and sexuality and the vitality and exuberance of engagement with activities we love, while the other is based on a sense of lack or deficiency. Eros, the Greek god of romantic and erotic love mentioned earlier, symbolizes the primordial desire that connects us to others, to community, and to the natural world. Eros also connects us to our own interior, drawing us into our inner world to embrace the deeper dimensions of ourselves.

Yet, eros can provoke the fear of too much experience, too much feeling, and even the fear of the superlative. Many of us evade the challenge of eros by reducing the full intensity of life to predictable patterns and familiar social roles. As if closing off the valve of our own life force, we either tamp down or disconnect from the fire element within us, leaving ourselves with a restricted feeling of little depth or intensity. This disconnection triggers the reflex to fill our hollowness with substitute forms of stimulation, such as sex, drugs, and rock 'n' roll. In this way our relationship with fire becomes neurotic, now expressed as deficiency desire.

Deficiency desire tries to fill in the psychic hole created by our disconnection from our naturally existing internal fire element because of our fear of its consuming intensity. Compensating for this separation, we're driven by the unconscious belief that we need continual gratification in order to camouflage our aching sense of boredom and emptiness. When the fire element is manipulated in the service of the ego or personality, we tend to focus only on what's positive and ego-reinforcing, while avoiding the opposite feelings of boredom, restlessness, and loneliness.

The fire element in its confused aspect commonly takes the form of obsession, seduction, and indiscriminate consumption of things, substances, or people, all of which promise to fill our emptiness and relieve us of our boredom. Ego co-opts the light of illumination and the heat of compassion to get us fired up on emotional highs. Advertising is a good metaphor for this confused form of desiring. It can seduce us to want things we don't really need, offering temporary satisfaction but ultimately leaving us empty and hungering for more.

Our desire becomes obsessive largely because we've forgotten who we are in our totality. We tend to come from only a part of ourselves rather than from our whole being. "You can never get enough of what you don't need" typifies deficiency desire, which stands in marked contrast to the left-hand approach to desire, which emerges from our wholeness, where all of us is present in our desiring.

In the laboratory of meditation, as we sit in silence and stillness, we can witness the mechanics of neurotic desire as it unfolds in the present moment. We can see that such desire is an expression of our dissatisfaction with the immediate instant. It's usually characterized by an underlying sense of restlessness, or energetic percolation—an inability to rest in simplicity.

We often don't accept the living moment as it is, but instead recruit desire to make nowness more interesting, more exciting, and more colorful—juicier. We manipulate the moment by thinking about it, having all kinds of ideas, associations, and feelings about what just arose in our mind. The Buddha spoke of this kind of desire in his teaching on the four noble truths, and identified it as the cause of suffering. It's wanting things to be different from the way they are. It's the unacknowledged thought "This is not it" or "This is not enough."

Not recognizing that we're manipulated by our underlying intolerance of boredom, we can't seem to get enough sensation, entertainment, or distraction. It's like staying up hours beyond our bedtime reading posts on Facebook, or having another glass of wine or another cigarette, or perhaps another slice of cheesecake while surfing the web. We want a little extra something so we take it to the limit one more time. The neurotic aspect of fire tends to scatter our attention as we get caught in a succession of unrelated details due to our fascination with thrilling surfaces that promise to captivate our attention.

Fulfilling deficiency desire doesn't quench the thirst of desire, but only feeds its driving force. We've been using our imagination, charm, and enthusiasm to prop up a sunny optimistic façade as protection from the pain of life's plateaus and valleys. We've been channeling the energy of fire into superficial playfulness and artificial enthusiasm to avoid the gray areas in our life. In doing so we employ fire in a neurotic way to hide from ourselves.

# 29

# The Shadow of Desire

Passion, pleasure, and seduction, as well as empathy, compassion, and creativity, comprise the emotional currency of our fire element. Fire's intense energy and vivid color symbolize youthful optimism, joy, and playfulness. It can spontaneously combust in sudden bursts of enthusiasm and exuberance, igniting a creative flight of ideas and visionary possibilities. But our love can also be seductive, superficial, and insatiable, and can jeopardize the very thing that we want most—to be loved. Fire is our friend, but it can blaze indiscriminately, destroying everything in its path. Its inflammatory nature also fuels aggressive acts and vengeful words, spreading ill will like wildfire and often ending in the ashes of destruction. As light always casts a shadow, the brightness and joyous energy of fire has a dark side.

Passion delivers us into relationship, but relationship becomes the great mirror from which we can't escape our own reflection. It challenges us to give up hiding and to surrender our hidden corners, to be fully visible before ourselves and before our intimate others. Yet, such exposure can provoke withdrawal as a way to preserve our inner world from visibility, intrusion, and judgment.

The fire of relationship confronts us with the core issues of human existence. Wanting to merge with another, and yet feeling the need to be independent, presents us with a curious paradox. Feeling loyal to our significant others while simultaneously experiencing the perverse pull to be free of such commitments is confusing. The tension between self-sacrifice and self-preservation causes ambivalence in our most intimate relationships.

We're so often caught in the paradox of feeling irresistibly drawn to the experience of intimacy and oneness, while equally desiring separation and independence. For many of us the impulse to become a separate, autonomous being is as strong as the desire to merge with a loved one.

The shadow of desire reveals division within ourselves and our struggle with ambivalence. The word *intimacy* comes from the Latin *intimus*, which means "intrinsic or essential and belonging to our deepest nature." We can't find genuine intimacy with spouses, family, and friends until we're intimate with ourselves, but this would involve communication with the very areas we've denied or ignored. Interestingly, to be a true *individual* means to not be divided, suggesting the integration of our many parts, many of which we've suppressed.

Romantic-erotic desire brings us into relationship with a beloved partner, where love dissolves the boundaries of separation and relieves us of our painful isolation. This stretching of our ego boundaries promotes our emotional growth, but in opening to a significant other we enter an unknown domain where we have to make friends with fear if we want to be truly intimate.

Authentic relationship is about openness and trust, connection and deep feeling, but the experience of temporary merger with another may threaten us with possible rejection, loss, and abandonment. If we dare drop our defenses and free fall into the mystery of love, our beloved might find us to not be enough, lacking in the substance necessary to sustain a relationship. The shadow of desire holds unreasonable and sometimes impossible expectations of our partners and loyal friends. Our idealization of particular people steals their right to be imperfect and incomplete, to lack the qualities we wish they had.

Many of us struggle with the fear of surrendering too much of ourselves to another, where we might become emotionally engulfed and lose our independence. There's also the anticipated disappointment that our beloved mate or our cherished friend won't be able to rescue us from our existential loneliness. Nor do they always mirror us when we urgently need support, which could leave us feeling even lonelier.

When we feel cut-off from the energy of our own fire element, the strategy of seduction seems necessary because we believe that we're missing the very qualities that would naturally earn other people's love and attention. This assumed lack is the basis of our self-deceptive shadow strategy to give love in order to get love. We don't believe that others will love us or pay attention to us as we truly are, and so we feel the need to draw people in to secure their attention, affection, and love.

Like flickering flames of fire, we're continually shape-shifting to satisfy the needs of others by focusing on what wins their attention and approval, but as a result we lose touch with our own depths and our own authenticity. Our neediness is camouflaged by our displays of enthusiasm, helpfulness, and generosity. The irony is that when we do receive love and affection it doesn't touch the core of our feeling of unworthiness. Our habit of moving away from feelings of boredom, loneliness, and emptiness has trapped us in the very feelings we're trying to avoid.

# 30

# The Fire Element's Personal Touch

When fire energy is dominant in our experience, we have natural charisma, a magnetic charm that captivates other people's attention and can lift their spirits with our infectious enthusiasm. Our intense energy, youthful optimism, and joy can also suddenly burst into a flight of creative ideas and visionary possibilities. Our virtue lies in our interpersonal skills and social intelligence, being intuitively aware of the motives and feelings of others as well as our own.

As we become aware that our strategy to manipulate our experiences was a symptom of estrangement from our inner fire, we reinhabit our body and are now willing to feel our heart, enabling us to genuinely empathize with other people's feelings, and to create lasting emotional bonds. Realizing that we don't have to shape the outcome of interactions with others to get attention and affection, we move from the surface to the depth of our relationships. We see that the love and affection we previously offered had an underlying expectation of reciprocity from others. By looking critically at our strategy to escape from pain, always seeking stimulating and enjoyable experiences, we can use our inner fire to illuminate the immediate reality of our undesirable feelings.

When we reconnect with our inner fire element, we can embrace the entire spectrum of our feelings without censoring them, which gives us the newfound ability to nurture ourselves. Using fire's discriminating wisdom we witness our tendency to escape from our darker emotions. No longer driven to grasp at the next stimulating experience or to present a charming persona, we're now available to experience our fears, conflicts, and insecurities.

By turning the light of compassion on ourselves, we can become intimate with our own interior, with our needs, fantasies, hopes, and fears. Only then can these denied aspects emerge safely in order to be integrated, affording us a sense of genuine wholeness. The wisdom of the fire element inspires us to appreciate the details of any situation or occasion without imagining how to make it even more enriching or exciting.

The neurotic distortion begins with our inadvertent disconnection from our fire energy due to our fear that it will illuminate our inner emptiness. Feeling the need to make up for this loss, we're now compelled to imitate its attributes by manipulating our experiences, trying to make them conform to what we imagine are fire's natural qualities. Highly defended against reexperiencing the original pain of our separation, we believe we have to stay positive, cheerful, and optimistic to camouflage the pain of our disconnection.

We strategize how to remain immune from experiencing emotional flatness by stimulating ourselves with fascinating and provocative ideas, sensory impressions, and the play of our vivid imagination. Any potentially painful experience is reframed or rationalized so that we don't have to experience negative feelings, which can feel like an assault on our persona-positive identity. Using our scintillating mind we distract ourselves from our depths, inadvertently losing touch with our own sense of authenticity.

Once fire energy is distorted, it depersonalizes our relationships with everyone and everything by reducing people and things to potentially pleasurable objects to consume. We're unable to fully appreciate anyone because we're using others to conceal our own emptiness. The more we feel that we're losing the presence of the other, the more we struggle to hold on in order to reassure ourselves that we're not alone.

Not believing that others will love us or pay attention to us as we truly are, we tend to become chameleonlike, manufacturing a pleasing façade to secure attention and affection. In the neurotic or distorted state fire energy displays itself as fascination with surface, image, presentation, and social packaging, and not genuine depth of feeling. Because we depend on others to give us what we can't give ourselves, we give love in order to get love.

Although we're full of outward gestures of love and affection in our relationships, in the neurotic state our love tends to be seductive, superficial, and insatiable. When we distort the energy of fire, we're more interested in ourselves than in others, and tend to convert friends and significant others into our captive audience. Our hunger for attention and affection can be disguised as a form of selfless love, which confirms our self-image as a wonderful partner and friend, but camouflages our real motivation.

When our relationship with fire is distorted, we don't easily tolerate emotional distance, as we're hypersensitive to emotional coldness and rejection. We grasp at others as if they could remedy our feeling of boredom and loneliness, only to experience short-lived gratification. We may soon lose interest and move on to the next person or experience glittering with promise. Trying to squeeze the last drop of pleasure out of everything, neurotic desire could take the form of addiction, but milder expressions are obsessions and entrenched patterns of craving stimulation, which offer only temporary self-forgetfulness.

Our distortion of fire's wisdom energy can fuel the creation of a self-image designed to get attention, love, and affection. Ironically, when we actually succeed in getting whom or what we thought we wanted, we might experience dissatisfaction because we want to be appreciated and loved for who we are, and not for our seductive self-image.

One of the significant problems when the fire element is dominant in our experience is that we can use our vivid imagination to idealize relationships, seeing the very best in others. Idealization can magnify everything wonderful about another, while denying the thorny issues in our relationships. Our idealized version of relationships not only allows us to avoid dealing with the troubling aspects of our friends and lovers, but prevents us from having a more revealing experience of the significant people in our life.

When we're willing to experience the full range of our feelings and be open to whatever life presents us, our strategic bubble of infectious optimism and cheerfulness gives way to a sense of gravitas and real substance. We now use fire's heat to extend the warmth of lovingkindness to ourselves, and fire's light to illuminate our unconscious habit of seeking entertaining stimuli.

The great challenge when the fire element predominates is finding enjoyment and meaning in plateau experiences, which are uneventful and emotionally neutral, and don't reinforce our charming self-image. This challenge entails deepening our capacity to trust what was formerly unlovable.

# 31

# Transforming Passion into Compassion

The primordial desire of Mother Nature inspires atoms to mate with one another to form molecules, and molecules to merge with one another to give birth to cells, and cells to embrace other cells to form tissues—and tissues to organs, and organs to organisms. Eros is the universal dance of love that draws complementary opposites together to give birth to the mind-boggling diversity of the phenomenal world.

Attraction is a fact of life. Without it there would be no binding force to hold our world together. Yet, passionate desire is a double-edged sword. It joins us with others, but can pierce our heart. It inflames our imagination with longing, tempting us to throw all care to the winds, but can stop us in our tracks with confusion and self-doubt. Caught between impulse and hesitation, we may not be sure how to go forward.

Imagine shopping in a favorite market. As we walk down the aisles with our cart, thinking of the items we need to purchase, suddenly we come face-to-face with a very attractive individual who looks at us with interest and smiles admiringly. We automatically return the smile but then avert our eyes, unsure of how long to linger in this vulnerable moment. Feeling the electricity of attraction—an increased pulse rate and a rise in bodily temperature—we begin to wonder what to do if we encounter this person again in the next aisle. Should we make ourselves available for a casual conversation or avoid such a possibility? Could this possibly lead to an exciting new friendship or an affair, or perhaps abruptly fall flat as quickly as it arose? By engaging in a conversation with a stranger, are we crossing a boundary that violates our primary relationship if we happen to be in one?

We're not trained in our culture how to creatively handle the electricity of desire. We tend either to suppress or dramatize this energy, hoping either to avoid the seduction of desire and its complications, or to impulsively fulfill our desires. But consider the possibility of just circulating the energy of attraction without shutting it down or acting it out. What if we allowed the magnetism of attraction to course through our body and mind without having to fulfill it in relationship with another person?

The left-hand method of working with desire doesn't always involve fulfilling desire but rather experiencing it. We take a moment to pause, dropping our attention from our head to our body to feel the electricity of attraction. Circulating the energy of desire can serve as a source of animation, vitality, and enhanced aliveness. The key is whether we've developed the willingness and capacity to appreciate and then *let go*.

In this case, letting go doesn't mean denying or rejecting, but releasing our psychological grip on the object of desire so that it's free from our emotional attachment. We caress and hold gently, and then let go mindfully, refraining from trying to capture the experience. In the scenario of the shopper in the aisle, our hold or grip could take the form of spinning a story about the current situation, or fanning the flame of our expectations, positive or negative, or allowing ourselves to get contaminated by old memories of success or failure.

Our usual confusion is a kind of vagueness—a lack of clarity—due to not recognizing what we're experiencing with specificity. Discernment—the virtue of the fire element—is the capacity to see with clarity and precision, so that we understand the implications of what we're experiencing in the moment. It cuts through the entanglement of our thoughts and memories to deliver us to what's actually happening as opposed to what we imagine. Whereas the water element objectively reflects the bare appearance of a particular situation, our inner fire enhances understanding, so that we can distinguish one quality or aspect from another, clarifying potential neurosis from sanity.

We might appreciate the admiring glance from the individual in the market as a reaffirmation that we're still attractive, and that we can still feel desire for another. We're not numb or disinterested, but have the courage to jump into the fray of life and take a chance, if we choose. Seeing clearly permits us the freedom to act rather than react based on previous conditioning.

The left-hand approach suggests that liberation involves a receptive openness to feelings of arousal, while simultaneously curbing the impulse to energetically pull in these sensations to central headquarters as our possession. We continue to stay open and receptive to the moment-by-moment unfolding of our experience, but we release our grip, again and again, trusting that the energy of passion is its own reward.

Allowing the force of desire to circulate, we enhance the quality of our aliveness by staying with the sensation of wanting while dropping the story line associated with the desire. This practice has bite to it because it feels unnatural or illogical to be deprived of our narrative about whom or what we desire. Yet, when we redirect our attention to the actual tone and texture of desire, we might discover that without our personal narrative our feelings are pure energy and hold surprising possibilities.

When we're not at a distance from what we're experiencing, we're fully there. With no sense of separation from our pleasure or our pain, our sensual delight or our experience of loss and grief, there's little motivation to be elsewhere. We might be surprised to find gratification where we least expect it.

The left-hand path recommends that rather than trying to superficially turn negative experiences into positive ones, we begin to look critically at our tendency to deny the raw, rugged, and unpredictable side of life by cultivating an overly one-sided optimism. We become mindful of how we shift immediately from pain to pleasure, from the immediate moment to the future, from feelings of vulnerability to *explaining* our vulnerability in order to create a sense of safety and certainty. As we develop confidence in the wisdom of our fire element, we no longer flee from feelings of emptiness, and we stop criticizing ourselves when we're not feeling happy, positive, or loved by another.

Through the fire element's discerning awareness we can discover the qualitative difference between samsara and nirvana. As we've discussed, samsara is the blinding force of collective conditioning that binds us to the wheel of repetitive patterns, and keeps us hankering after a better moment than the one we're already experiencing. Seeing precisely how samsara works, and why it works the way it does, illuminates its mechanism. The recognition and understanding of how neurotic or deficiency desire manifests, how it functions, and how it gets us to mindlessly repeat ourselves—and how it prevents us from seeing—is precisely what liberates us.

The light of discriminating awareness recognizes and understands the diverse and contradictory aspects of ourselves, while the heat of the fire element holds them with love and appreciation. This involves honoring the contradictory parts of us—the part of us that longs to be in a committed relationship as well as the part of us that fears such relationships, the part of us that's needy and dependent as well as the part of us that's strenuously independent.

This combination of light and warmth, of recognition and embrace, allows our many dimensions to be integrated within our personality so that we can accept the ambiguity and complexity of ourselves, the imperfection of all relationships, while being able to offer ourselves to another without the fear of losing ourselves.

# 32

# What Buddha Might Recommend

Set aside some time to experience the wisdom energy of the fire element.

## Fire Element Meditation 1

Begin by taking a seated position, and bring your attention to the rhythmic cycle of your breathing in a relaxed manner. After five to ten minutes, when you feel you're settled, visualize bright white light emanating from your out-breath. During the in-breath you don't visualize anything. The light represents love and compassion, which you initially radiate to loved ones, but then to acquaintances or individuals you feel neutral about. You also can include the nonhuman world of animals, mountains, forests, clouds, waterfalls, and turquoise oceans. Part of the visualization is to imagine the recipients of your love being positively affected.

After a number of these sessions, when you feel confident in doing this practice, try to include your adversaries—those individuals for whom you have negative feelings. These could be people who are presently in your life, or people with whom you've had conflict in the past. By being able to include your adversaries, your expression of compassion becomes unlimited.

## Fire Element Meditation 2

Begin by assuming a comfortably seated position, and feel yourself physically present. Making no effort to control your breathing, bring your attention to the rhythmic cycle of breathing in a relaxed and light-handed manner.

After five minutes, either look at an actual image or conjure up an image of a person, thing, or scenario that stimulates desire, the unmistakable feeling of "I want." Continue to focus on this person or object until you really feel the pull of desire. Pay particular attention to how desire shows up in your body, perhaps as an increase in heart rate, a heightening of bodily tension, or a rise in bodily temperature.

As you imagine coming closer to the chosen person, or possessing the desirable object, or luxuriating in a much-desired situation, instead of grasping at or merging with the object of your desire try to feel only appreciation and love for its attractive qualities.

Desire pulls the person or thing or situation toward us, or us toward it, with an expectation of gratification. Compassion or appreciation radiates outward away from ourselves, without an expectation of personal gratification. In this meditative exercise we're not trying to substitute one for the other, but rather to recognize the difference in quality between compassion and desire.

## Practical Applications

Here are some domains where we can work with the fire element through the practice of contemplation. These challenging contemplative exercises will be most rewarding if you commit your thoughts to journal writing.

### Motivation

In this contemplative exercise you're going to consult with the wise old man or woman who has already lived your life. This ancient wise one lives within you and has profound insight into what you have essentially lived for.

Assuming this profound perspective, inquire what is the core desire beneath all of your desires. In other words, are you motivated by an overarching life purpose that energizes you, is your primary motivation driven by the desire to live a normal life, to marry and have a family, or to work at a satisfying job, or are you just trying to get through another week?

You might consider whether you're primarily motivated by the quest for personal development, the desire for adventure or entertaining experiential possibilities, the wish for recognition and admiration from others, or the desire to promote the welfare of others? Do you trust the directionality of your life journey or not?

### Sexuality and love

(A) Inquire whether you're in touch with your own sexuality. Is your sexual activity creative, spontaneous, playful, tender, and loving, or do you check out, going on automatic pilot in the midst of sexual activity? Do you inhibit yourself due to morality, past conditioning, or trauma? Is there a discrepancy between how you picture yourself in your sexual fantasies and how you behave sexually with your partner? What do you imagine would support your free, uninhibited sexual expression?

(B) Are you involved in relationships where it's natural to express love, care, and compassion? Are your loving relationships mutual with an equivalency of give-and-take? In your loving relationships are you willing to give for the sake of the other without always receiving gratification? Does your love extend to the nonhuman world, including animals and nature? Do you take time to appreciate music, literature, art, and other enjoyable activities?

### Friendships

Do you distinguish between friendships and acquaintances? What criteria do you base your friendships upon? Do you have a community of friends with whom you keep in close contact? When encountering conflicts or disagreements, do you find yourself blending with others, going up against them, or emotionally distancing yourself from them? When relationships are no longer gratifying or meaningful, are you willing to invest energy to move beyond where they're stuck? Do you find the courage to move on from a relationship that you've outgrown?

# Part Five

# Wind Element:
# Circulation of Energy and Kinetic Movement

With increasing confidence in the power of our natural rhythms, we take pleasure in completing tasks and accomplishing goals that give shape to our life. By living in alignment with our inner wind and going along with its intelligent flow, we invite the freedom of meaningful coincidence.

**Qualities**
Courage and confidence
Playfulness, patterns of orderly chaos
Mastery and excellence
Energy, vigor, vitality
Karmic cause and effect
Meaningful coincidence or synchronicity

# 33

# If Wind Could Speak

I am the breath of life, the all-pervading rhythm of the universe, in which creation and destruction follow each other like the alternating tides of your breathing. All movement, change, and transformation are my doing, as I'm the principle of energetic force and activity. You will find me in the purposeful movement that follows from your intentions, in the mental process of envisioning a goal, and in the activity that brings it to completion.

Through the circulation of your inner wind embodied in your nervous system, I bring you sensations from the outer world so that you can see things from different perspectives and move in new directions. I'm most pleased when you listen deeply to your own depths and attune yourself to your inner vibrations. By doing so, you draw situations to yourself that are in accordance with these vibrations. From this alignment you magnetize meaningful coincidences, where outer circumstances spontaneously coincide with your immediate state of mind.

I'm displeased when you disconnect from your own wind energy, for then you're drawn to be compulsively on the go, endlessly busy with tasks, projects, and the urgent need to achieve goals, but without lasting satisfaction.

On the other hand, if you open to the natural circulation of my life force, epitomized by your breath, you will allow situations to unfold naturally. You'll feel as if you're dancing in the wind of circumstances, as you experience accomplishment without struggle. Virtue is found in trusting my natural rhythms and going along with their intelligent flow.

Like the totality of nature where all parts move together in one orchestrated movement, when you're in alignment with my energy you'll be able to ride the currents of your life without doubt or hesitation.

# 34

# Dancing with the Wind

The continual force of wind carves landscapes, bends cypress trees like bonsai plants, etches marvelous patterns in lime and sandstone boulders, and designs desert dunes into shifting structures of elegance. The element of wind symbolizes the circulation of life force throughout the natural world, as in summer when all of nature is fiercely active and fulfilling its functions, but also as evidenced by the rhythmic rising and falling of the oceanic tides and the progression of the seasons. In the animal kingdom wind incarnates as instinct, infallibly guiding the round of feeding and fighting, mating and nurturing, birth and death.

The virtue of the wind element in the Buddhist mandala is the wisdom of all-accomplishing action. This virtue is somewhat paradoxical because life is already accomplished, epitomized by the natural cycle of breathing, which happens without strategy or effort. Our breathing is a microcosm of this circulation of life force, as we and the rest of the natural world are rhythmically breathed by the universe. Like a huge cosmic web, the force of life embraces the infinitely small and infinitely large within its network of interdependent relations. The wisdom energy of the wind element is a great benefactor, and we're the recipients of this goodness. We discover virtue by trusting the natural rhythms of our life and going along with their intelligent flow. The energy of the wind element not only serves our survival, but guides us to develop a sense of life direction and purpose.

Inner wind is the circulation of energy throughout the meridians of our subtle body, the highly sensitive body beneath our flesh and bones. The inner wind is expressed through our nervous system, which brings us sensations from the outer world so that we can move toward things with purposeful behavior, connecting sensory information with action. The ability to ride or dance with unfolding situations requires the play of both the masculine and feminine principles of wind energy, which we all possess.

The masculine version of wind energy is the thrusting movement of fearlessly advancing forward, cutting through the obstacles of tangential thought and frivolous behavior. It expresses itself as the skillful use of personal power. Masculine wind energy is efficient and effective and moves forward with the diligence to make projects materialize. It's also positively combustible behavior, as air mixed with the fire of desire makes flames burn brighter with intensity. Wind energy inspires the feeling that we can accomplish anything because of our wholehearted involvement.

Activity, growth, speed, efficiency, and achievement are the language of the masculine aspect of the wind element, but so is the movement of thought and the functioning of the intellect. The mental process of going from a goal to an actual plan, bringing projects to completion, symbolizes our use of will and intentionality—a directed or purposeful movement that makes things take shape. Wind is the psychic force that allows our mind to move in new directions and to see things from different perspectives. This rational, inquisitive, and piercing aspect of masculine wind energy is symbolized by the sword, which can cut through delusions and complicated problems.

The feminine expression of wind is our willingness to open to the natural circulation of life force, epitomized by our breath and the circulation of our blood. It's the rhythmic movement natural to organic life, as manifested in the undulating movements of sexual activity, giving birth, and the peristaltic movement of swallowing.

When we're aligned with the rhythms of our own wind energy, and when our mind and body are synchronized—in one place at one time—we hum like a well-tuned engine, expressing resonance, harmony, and balance. From this balanced perspective we find ourselves in alignment with the ordinary magic of everyday situations as we meet the energy of the moment and ride its currents.

In the movie *American Beauty*, there's a remarkable scene where one of the characters films a plastic bag swirled by the wind in a kind of mini-cyclone. The wind gathers leaves that have been scattered on the pavement, sweeping them along with the bag in one synchronized movement. The plastic bag and the leaves dance effortlessly, like animate beings at play, in mesmerizing twists and turns, dips and pivots, creating a stunning display. In a poetic moment, the young photographer states that in observing this magical play he was so overwhelmed with the benevolent force of life and the world's beauty that he knew he was not alone, and had no reason to ever fear again.

This scene beautifully captures the wind element moving effortlessly as if along invisible power lines. All of us have had moments when we've experienced serendipitous occasions, when things came together effortlessly and gracefully. During these moments we might have felt as though our head, heart, and belly and the immediate surroundings were all sympathetically connected with one another.

When we and our world are attuned we invite auspicious or favorable circumstances to occur, a coinciding of situations with our immediate state of mind. Such coincidences give us the feeling that we and the situations we find ourselves in are part of the same tapestry. At such times we might feel as if we were woven into the immense design of things. When our inner wind or life force circulates without the distorting influence of our monkey mind, we feel a greater sense of intimacy and belonging. Even painful experiences such as a dear friend becoming chronically ill or dying, or a loving relationship falling apart, can also bring us an unexpected sense of intimacy with life. With such a head-on collision with life, we might intuitively understand that a momentum of forces and energies delivered us and others to this sharp-edged moment and dropped the bottom out from our life. Yet, we're inclined to benignly accept such a turn of events because somehow they feel lawful and appropriate. Although painful, we find ourselves participating in an unfolding that's larger than our individual life. Such moments can be strangely gratifying.

We're either driven by the wind of circumstances or we're like the plastic bag dancing in the wind. We either feel in conflict with the way things are and resist the current, or we creatively navigate the winds of circumstances, allowing situations and relationships to unfold naturally. Stepping mindfully into the turbulent waters of life we can move along with their currents without trying to control them; at the same time we honor our own inclinations by steering ourselves to promote what's optimal.

# 35

# Breath as the Sacred Marriage of Masculine and Feminine

We read in the Old Testament that God scooped up earth and fashioned a human being, then blew the breath of life into Adam, circulating divine substance and energy in our primal ancestor. Breath is the movement of primordial life force that animates not only human beings but all of life. As we tune into the natural rhythmic cycle of breathing, it may occur to us that all beings and things, from whales to wallabies, from supernovas to quarks, are moving, changing, and transforming themselves as part of one common flow.

What could be more obvious than breath? Although we've been breathing since the day of our birth, precious few of us realize that each and every breath is entirely new. In the Buddhist tradition, when we bring awareness to what's most immediate and near, our breath invites us into a virgin state of psychological nakedness where we're momentarily free of our habitual behavior patterns.

We can employ the cycles of breathing to remind us to feel into the tone and texture of whatever situation is immediately unfolding, trusting that life's intelligence will lead us to what's next. Fresh perspectives and possibilities seem to emerge out of nowhere. Imagine walking aimlessly in a field of freshly fallen snow, the crisp crunching sound of every step bringing us delight, as does the hummingbird who suddenly appears at the feeder in our garden. Looking into the eyes of a loved one we might see something we've never noticed before as we're filled with wonder. We only have to show up and our life is already accomplished without struggle. This is the virtue of the feminine aspect of wind.

On the other hand, if we've lingered too long in a safe place, life may suddenly pull the bottom out from under us, sending us into a free fall. If we've been inflated with self-importance, life may puncture our bubble of self-intoxication. And if we've been speeding through our days, juggling too many activities, physical depletion or illness might bring us face-to-face with the parts of ourselves we've been avoiding. This is the masculine aspect of wind, which cuts through whatever obstacles hold us in mind-numbing repetitive patterns.

As we bring awareness to the natural rhythm of our breathing, we realize that the maddening affair of changes isn't haphazard, but has its own intelligent pattern. The cycle of breathing, like the circulation of blood, the elliptical orbit of the planets, and the orderly progression of the seasons, seems to be part of one cosmic current. This feminine aspect of the wind intuitively realizes that we and the rest of the world are rhythmically breathed, and that movement has a pattern.

The cycles of breathing whisper the message that if we want a fresh breath, we first surrender the breath that we're presently holding. Unless we exhale, we won't be able to draw a fresh inhalation. Such sacrifice echoes a natural law with bite to it, especially when we find that we have to let go of someone whom we've been holding onto dearly, to make way for what's next in our life as well as theirs.

We're notorious for secretly demanding that situations conform to our fixed ideas of them. We live with an unreasonable insistence that people and things should be different than the way they already are. Bringing awareness to our breathing aligns us with the natural rhythm of beginnings and endings, reminding us to let go into the stream of change. The masculine aspect of wind is the confidence to use power or kinetic force to break up our holding patterns, permitting a free flow of energy.

Inhaling the intoxicating fragrance of this magnolia blossom, we'd love to savor its fragrance unendingly, but in trying to hold it, we lose it. Its aroma is intoxicating only when it freely circulates; it evaporates when held. We can't truly hold onto anything, in the sense of making it our personal possession, even what's most precious and desirable. With an adult mind and the innocence of a child, we might realize that the ordinary cycles of breathing are modeling for us that we can't hold onto the nearest and dearest people in our life—not to spouses, children, parents, or the most exquisite experiences. They're passing, and so are we, moving irresistibly in the stream of time. The feminine aspect of wind inspires us to let go, reminding us that the shadow of impermanence makes these experiences ever so precious.

This awareness could provoke sadness and despair, and threaten our sense of safety and security. It's all too human to want to cherish whom and what we love without end, but as we learn to both hold and release continually like the movement of breath, we can trust that new life follows from death. In this way we integrate both masculine and feminine aspects of wind energy.

Breathing is a doorway leading to that which transcends us. With each breath, we draw from a vast boundless atmosphere that connects us umbilically to what's not us. Our very life, moment by moment, is sustained by what lies outside of us, and yet without that "other," we could not be. The continuous cycles of breath remind us that something larger than us holds all of it. If we had to assume responsibility for the process of breathing, we would have died shortly after birth. There's a larger energetic pattern, an interconnected web within which life occurs, one that maintains and sustains us. We're being breathed by the totality of life, which lives through us, transforming us into a mysterious being infinitely larger than our personality and our personal history.

# 36

# The Trap of Compulsive Busyness

When we begin to mistrust the natural unfolding of our life, we disconnect from our inner wind energy and are likely to experience feelings of groundlessness, insecurity, and anxiety. As with the other elements, when we rupture our connection with their vital energy we try to replicate their natural qualities by mimicking their intelligent and graceful movement, but in a distorted manner. In the case of the wind element, we forcibly direct it through compulsive achievement and overlapping activities, as if trying to stave off anxiety by keeping busy.

Like the wind when it moves in mini-cyclones, going over the same territory again and again, our neurotic relationship with our wind energy involves compulsively juggling multiple activities and endlessly organizing things, while attempting to keep up with the continual changes in our life. Attempting to pacify ourselves, we channel our anxiety and agitation into one project after another, but ironically we find ourselves dogged by the feeling that our goals and projects are still getting ahead of us. The more preoccupied we are with order and control, success and achievement, the more clearly defined chaos and failure become. When strategic thinking and obsession with achievement replace feeling and openness, we lose contact with the felt sense of our body and our surroundings.

The underlying fear of incompetence, insufficiency, and failure may begin to dominate our thoughts, and the suspicion that others are getting ahead of us causes more agitation. The more we feel apprehensive that we won't be able to keep up with life's demands, the faster we hurry and the more we feel like we're sinking, like being in quicksand. Although we may be functioning quite well we're gripped by the painful and sometimes paralyzing doubt that we won't be able to achieve our life goals in our ever-diminishing lifetime. Yet, the thrill of anticipated success and the fear of failure—the compulsion to create order and the threat of it all coming undone—provide us with an edge of excitement and reinforce the blindness of these patterns.

Feeling that we can't afford to relax, we struggle to stay on top of our ever-mounting tasks and projects so that we don't fall behind. Because of the emphasis we place on staying ahead of an imagined accelerating curve, the feeling of impending disorder and failure is accentuated. This fear is frequently denied, which then creates the need for constant overlapping activity to conceal our underlying anxiety.

When we camouflage our underlying fear, anticipating everything that could go wrong, we tend to project a battlefield situation of "us versus them," which justifies the need for continual suspicion and self-defense. The speed and aggression of wind neurosis provides a sense of having an edge, which keeps us sharp and vigilant and gives us the deceptive feeling that we're advancing forward.

The hidden aspect of wind energy is the nagging feeling that we need to continually defend ourselves from external threats, maintained by the belief that the world is a chaotic and dangerous place. We're well defended against any hint of our own incompetence or inability to succeed. This in turn could give rise to hypervigilance and an overreaction to imagined threats to our safety and security.

Yet, there are unavoidable periods in our life when we do experience failure or inadequacy, or when we face the inner doubt that we could've done better. We might be plagued with the feeling that we didn't reach our ideal of personal achievement, that we could've worked harder to achieve a more meaningful and gratifying livelihood, or that we should've changed careers when we had a chance to do so. We may feel a sense of failure because the love has gone out of our marriage, or our parenting skills have proven insufficient to prevent one of our children from dropping out of college or from becoming an addict or an alcoholic.

One of the methods of the left-hand path is to sensitively listen to our own depths. Such deep listening attunes us to the movement of our inner wind, where we find guidance for how to use failure and defeat, victory and success, to bring about transformation. It's as if there were a gravitational force that's drawing our many parts and the many aspects of our life into alignment toward potential wholeness. By living in alignment with our inner wind and by connecting with our heart, we finally realize that we have primary value independent of what we achieve.

An important question to ask ourselves is whether we lose heart when we feel defeated by circumstances. How we handle our experience of failure is crucial. On the other side of the coin, although we might be successful in various domains of our life, another important question to ask is whether our successes have deepened our understanding, moved us closer to our core, closer to our authentic purpose in life. Have we used our failures or successes as catalysts to transform ourselves, or have they simply reinforced our identification as a winner or a struggling loser?

# 37

# Befriending the Demon of Anxiety

The demon or neurotic aspect of the wind element is restlessness, agitation, and anxiety. It's the feeling of being ridden by circumstances rather than feeling like the rider. On the other hand, when we intuitively sense that there's a dance between ourselves and the events that are unfolding in the moment, we're inspired to pay attention to the peculiar patterns of our everyday experience. It might be the subtle change of facial expression of our boss, the momentary whiff of body fragrance of our spouse, or an abrupt shift in the energy of a room full of people. As we learn to tune into the energy of ordinary circumstances, we're immediately connected to the wind element's circulation of power. Such sensory attunement joins us to the world.

Most situations pulsate with energy and have texture, tone, and a style of movement. Energy can be smooth and flowing, a trickle or an avalanche, or at other times feel like a staccato, percolating, expansive, or contracting movement. As we feel into the tone and texture of situations as they unfold, we learn to ride their currents by paying attention to the pattern and direction of the energy itself. There's a reciprocal relationship between us and the world.

We can intuitively know when and how to pacify a chaotic situation, how to enrich an emotionally flat or uneventful situation, when it's time to magnetize others who are holding back, or how and when to cut through a situation that's become unnecessarily complicated or destructive. For example, imagine being in a coffee shop when a disheveled and disoriented homeless man walks in and sits down at a table without having ordered anything. The other patrons can't help but notice that something is disturbed and disturbing about this individual.

Already agitated and anxious, the homeless man becomes increasingly tense as he notices that others are distancing themselves from him.

As an expression of the wind element, instead of only feeling compassion for this homeless person, we might intuitively sense what compassion wants to do. We could ride the energy of compassion by addressing the homeless man with the simple question: "How're you doing this evening? If you're short on change, I'd be happy to get you something." In this way we spontaneously pacify or soothe this man by knowing what to offer to bring down the energy of agitation and alienation. This isn't a mind-constructed strategy but rather an intuitive sensing of the situation.

At other times, perhaps at work or at a social gathering, we might encounter individuals who can't find their own voice because of insecurity or diminished self-esteem. Aligning ourselves with our inner wind energy, we're bodily moved to correct the imbalance by feeling into their insecurity and hesitation. We enrich or cultivate such individuals by affirming them—by validating their basic human worthiness—so that they feel they have an emotional foundation. We might involve them by getting their input: "I wonder if you'd be willing to share your thoughts about this issue over lunch. I've heard you speak in the past about this topic, and I'd appreciate your perspective." Beyond a problem-solving mentality, we're spontaneously moved to provide safety, support, and nurturance by encouraging others to recognize their own worth.

Some people are introverted and introspective, preferring to operate under the radar or behind the scenes. They may be afraid of criticism and tend to make themselves small and socially invisible. Feeling into our own wind energy we intuitively position ourselves so that we're invited to enter their personal space and join with their energetic field. We might spontaneously magnetize such individuals by enlisting their aid or requesting their support, thereby eliciting their capacities and strengths. We enable them to come out from hiding and to feel confident about showing up.

There's a very shy person in our Buddhist community who rarely expresses herself, but lets her boyfriend speak on her behalf. I intentionally enlisted her as my retreat assistant. Although she's incredibly shy in person, she proved to be a brilliant assistant administrator and was able to communicate clearly by email. Through the opportunity to assist, she was able to discover her power and feel more confident about her ability to function independently.

The most difficult situation to work with is aggression. We might encounter someone who's so full of himself that he's sucking all the oxygen out of the room. He's either completely oblivious to whether others are interested in his inflated bravado, or he simply couldn't care less. We and others might feel hemmed in by the dictates of social decorum, believing that we have to accommodate this situation. The challenge of the left-hand approach is learning how to make use of the tension between the inhibitions of social convention and our urge to impulsively express our irritation.

That tension, if held with awareness, might abruptly spark a direction, a movement out of the impasse.

The subjugating aspect of wind energy, in this case, could take the form of not giving our undivided attention to this individual. Instead, we anchor ourselves in our own body by feeling its energy. Perhaps we suddenly change the topic of conversation, or recruit others to speak, or order food to shift the atmosphere. We might break the flow of this person's conversation by abruptly asking him how his food tastes, bringing his attention back down into his body and his senses. This cuts his frivolous and inflated energy without our having to criticize him.

We ride the wind of the situation by grounding ourselves in the tangible experience of our own energy. Without self-consciousness we cut through this individual's arrogance and inflation by not giving him any reinforcement, leaving him with his own empty echo. Navigating the currents of changing circumstances is possible when we're willing to engage in activities wholeheartedly, with our whole being, and not out of a particular agenda or to achieve a specific result. Such passionate involvement allows us to enjoy the game of life without having to win.

# 38

# The Wind Element's Personal Touch

When we're in alignment with the natural energy of wind, we have the confidence to act without self-doubt and the capacity to persevere when things are difficult. The wisdom of wind gives us the ability to distinguish ego-reinforcing accomplishment from actions that are expressions of our genuine personhood. This manifests as the character strength of courage to accomplish goals in the face of opposition, without shrinking from challenge or difficulty.

We can recognize the basic difference between our authentic self and the role of being a performance-oriented individual. Witnessing how we've previously substituted action for genuine feeling, we now challenge the mentality of win or lose, gain or loss, success or failure, as we passionately involve ourselves in activities that express our genuine needs and desires. Because we're synchronized with our world we realize that we don't make things happen as independent actors separate from the natural unfolding of situations. Our projects are brought to completion by moving with the intelligent flow of life's natural rhythms.

Distinguishing between actions that defend us from our feelings and those that spring from our core, when we're in tune with the wisdom energy of wind, we're able to appreciate the value of feelings, even the painful feelings of failure and loss, or inadequacy and incompetence. We've learned to extend lovingkindness to ourselves independent of personal achievement, and so we're willing to be vulnerable to another and surrender ourselves in intimate relationships. Living in attunement with our inner wind we dive into relationships with vitality and vigor, excitement and enthusiasm.

Yet, our relationship with our inner wind can become

neurotic when we disconnect from our own depths. Mistaking our image of competence and success for the total human being that we are, we sacrifice communicating with our own interior in favor of the tangible rewards that outer activities provide. Consequently, our sense of self doesn't arise from deep contact and communication with our interior but rather conforms to the constructed image of someone who gets things done. We're so caught up in compulsive doing that we distract ourselves from seeing who we really are at our depth.

Loss and failure are simply a part of the fabric of human life. When we lack trust in the journey that is our life, we're driven to strenuously create ourselves out of some idealization of who we think we should be. Believing that we are what we do, we place enormous emphasis on action and striving to do things well, but as a consequence we may suffer a conspicuous lack of interest in our own interior world.

Lacking such trust, we might lose the confident expectation that our life has an intelligent momentum and will evolve naturally. Consequently, we're driven to strenuously create ourselves through effortful activity. Tangible achievements become a misguided effort to compensate for this rupture from our inner wind element. We believe that doing takes precedence over feelings, which we regard as inconveniences on the way to achievement and success.

The demon of the wind element, when our relationship with it has become distorted, is the threat of failure, which provokes restlessness, agitation, and inner drivenness. Viewing others as competitors for shrinking resources, hypervigilance, obsessive thinking, workaholism, competition, and control deflect attention away from our fear of inner emptiness. In the uninspected state we often react with the compensatory need for tangible proof of our worthiness, and this renews another cycle of neurotic wind.

The accomplishment of goals and tasks, and the completion of projects, takes primary importance, often displaying itself in a spirit of competition and winning. Constantly busy, both internally and externally, we believe that without our dedicated effort to control both ourselves and our environment, our life would meander aimlessly and nothing would ever get done.

Remarkably, because of the enormous emphasis we place on action and striving to do things well, we fall into the trap of regarding feelings, body-based sensitivity, and intuition as foreign territory. When we're disconnected from our feelings, we could be insensitive to other people's feelings as we try to control them, or at our worst, we might be ruthless in our ambition to succeed in a particular endeavor and step over others on the way toward our destination.

The greater the gap between outer goals and objectives and our interior subjective world, the more we inadvertently create a chasm within ourselves. This painful perception of inner emptiness often propels us into ever more activity. The more emphasis we place on keeping in constant motion or successfully juggling many activities, the more resistant we become to experiencing our darker feelings of failure, loss, and insecurity. Constant activity serves as a temporary defense against suppressed feelings that might inconveniently emerge to slow us down.

When under the influence of wind energy, we're highly kinetic, but in the neurotic state the way we valorize competency and success above all else compromises our capacity to genuinely love and care for others. Focused largely on self-control as well as the control of others, we find the invitation to give ourselves to an intimate other very challenging because of our fear of being controlled.

Our skill and capacity to get things done can make us indispensable to our friends and loved ones, but the role itself takes precedence over our capacity for loving. We could find ourselves acting out our preconception of intimate partnership or friendship, but then when we do receive love, we might wonder whether it was our competencies that earned love rather the genuine person beneath our functions and roles. In order to feel anchored in our authentic self, we need to be willing to experience the full range of our feelings and realize that who we are isn't the same as what we do.

# 39

# Inviting Meaningful Coincidence

In the Buddhist mandala, the virtue of the wind element—the wisdom of all-accomplishing action—isn't based on achieving goals, either worldly or spiritual. There's no longer a struggle to be anyplace other than where we find ourselves, and no need to be a better self than the one we presently are. We begin to realize that the ordinary world is already sacred, complete, and uncontaminated. But we do need to participate in our life, which means being willing to communicate intimately with ourselves and allowing the world to communicate directly with us.

On the left-hand path we practice "listening" to our internal vibrations and those in our environment. When we strike a pair of tuning forks, each gradually matches the vibrational frequency of the other, establishing resonance. Likewise, inner listening joins our mind and body, our heart and soul, and promotes a more harmonious relationship with our world. We draw to ourselves or are drawn to particular circumstances that coincide with our internal state. In this sense, we can ride the energy of situations and everyday occasions as an expression of our alignment with the world. Creatively riding the energy of circumstances is the basis of all accomplishing activity, the virtue of the wind element.

My spiritual teacher embodied a sacred view and was a master of attuning himself to the atmospheric energy of everyday situations. While giving a talk to a group of several hundred, whether he was drinking sake, adjusting his glasses, or reaching for a Japanese fan on his small table, he'd caress the chosen object very intentionally, as if he were regarding it for the first time. He might even pause before sipping his beverage and sniff the contents. He would sip very slowly and return the glass to the table very methodically. There would be a pause. He would simply sit in complete and total presence, and then after several minutes he'd begin speaking.

The speed and restlessness of those in the audience would progressively slow down. Everyone's attention would become more refined, more attuned to the vivid details in the environment. Unknown to the audience, their internal vibration or wind energy was synchronizing itself with this master teacher's energy. Having taken his seat properly, with confidence and dignity, poised between heaven and Earth, he had delivered his message before uttering a word.

We invite synchronicity or meaningful coincidence by living in intimate relationship with our interior and by appreciating the details of ordinary activities.

It's like having a good day when we feel centered in ourselves and notice that we seem to be experiencing a higher incidence of serendipitous events. We step out into the world and the door opens for us, as opposed to a day when we feel imbalanced and in conflict, a time when the world meets us with its jagged edges.

When we initially relate with our wind energy, we're working with the intelligent current of life force within our own body. Wind is the energy of vibration and movement, but also sound and communication among and between all of our parts. If we disconnect from parts of ourselves that we judge as threatening or disturbing, or ignore parts that we feel are insignificant, the whole system becomes imbalanced.

On a physical or organic level, each of our organs is talking to every other organ through electrical impulses and chemical messages. If our heart stops speaking to our lungs, or our pancreas resists communicating with our stomach, or if the communication is misunderstood, a breakdown occurs within the entire mind-body system. The networks of communication within the body promote integration, balance, and wholeness, but any breach in their conversation causes dis-ease, imbalance, and suffering.

On an emotional level, when we grieve the loss of someone very dear to us, we surrender control, feeling the pain in our heart as we give in to weeping. Perhaps we speak out loud to this loved one, expressing our sorrow and confessing any misgivings in our relationship with them. Eventually the energetic winds of bereavement become softer, perhaps even a murmur. By contrast, wanting to put the loss of this beloved friend or relative behind us, we might let ourselves get totally absorbed in the distracting business of everyday life in order to avoid contact with our underlying grief. Our unshed tears might eventually manifest as a major depression, or psychosomatic illness signaling that we've ruptured the circuit of communication with a significant part of us.

We all experience emotional knots or impasses in our life, the feeling of being stuck without an obvious exit. Whether in our marriage or our friendships, our business or our financial situation, from time to time our energy stagnates and we can't seem to move forward. The left-hand path encourages us to be *in* the impasse. By taking a seat in the subtle pulsation of our inner wind without trying to remedy the problem, our listening can become deeper and more refined. This practice begins by dropping our personal story and then directing our attention to our body, to the energy of our sensations and feelings.

For instance, we might be preoccupied with a number of issues and concerns involving our parents, our home, or our work, which sit like heavy weights on our chest and feel like knots in our head. By feeling our way into these energetic knots we begin communicating with the subtle layers of our mind-body. As we tune into the energetic dimension of experience, we open to the vibration or resonance, tone, and subtle texture of our situation. We pay acute attention to how we're breathing, to the lines of tension or numbness in our body, to the contraction in the pit of our stomach, or the pounding in our temples. Each of these symptoms reveals our resistance to accepting a personal truth, and going with the flow.

As we release the holding patterns of these energetic knots, our symptoms gradually become less intense and of less duration. When not framed by our problematic narrative they return to being liberated movements of energy in the open space of our mind-body. We might, for example, suddenly realize that it's time to call our estranged father and let him know that we love him, in spite of wounds between us. Or an elegant image of our living room might suddenly appear to us, clarifying how to transform the stale decor of our old house into something refreshing. We might tune into just how exhausted we are from our work, and immediately recognize that it's time for a restorative vacation. Our mind abruptly shifts, and some hidden part of ourselves reveals itself. Like a gust of wind that clears the air, a subtle change of perspective may occur. We discover the wisdom of the wind element in its continuous circulation of energy and its spontaneous shifting of direction.

The magic of tuning into or listening to our inner winds allows us to experience a meaningfulness in unexpected coincidences as if they were a link, a sympathetic connection between the outer event and our interior state. While walking through our city or town at night, a stray cat bolts out from an alley, looks up at us, and meows plaintively, perhaps mirroring our own feelings of loneliness; the vividness of a wildflower growing out of the crack in a sidewalk pierces our bubble of preoccupation, reminding us of the unstoppable force of life animating us; or an infant's open-eyed gaze and innocent smile captures our attention and melts our heart, refreshing our own sense of innocence and basic goodness.

Such moments feel strangely intimate, as if speaking to unacknowledged parts of ourselves. They also feel favorable or auspicious because they startle us into a recognition of an outer event that feels relevant to our immediate state of mind.

When we sit down to our morning bowl of granola, we could take a few moments to consider that the momentum of our entire life brought us to this immediate occasion of enjoying our breakfast. We could've found ourselves in very unpleasant circumstances, but instead the universe offered to us this precious moment. We happen to be at the right spot at the right time to enjoy this meal. In order for that grain to be in our bowl, millions of flora and fauna had to die and get recycled in the nitrogen cycle of the soil. The sun had to shine from a distance of approximately 93 million miles to promote the growth of oat crops. If the sun were a little too close or too far away, our planet would either be a lifeless desert or a globe of ice. Water had to evaporate from oceans, lakes, and streams, and rise up as mist, only to fall back down to Earth as rain, rejuvenating the soil and the crops of oats.

With this kind of big thinking, we might now eat our morning bowl of granola with appreciation, taking immense delight in this simple act. Our enjoyment seems to come out of nowhere, yet this benevolent experience coincides with our reverent state of mind. This contemplative practice can include bathing, working, dining with friends and family, conversation, and aimless wandering through our city or town.

Eventually we move gracefully along with the naturally occurring rhythms of situations, unbound by the karmic law of cause and effect. Instead of feeling trapped in a linear sequence of causal events, like a line of falling dominoes, we experience the occasions and events of our life as a spontaneous unfolding of themes that are outer expressions of what's implicit in our depths.

We invite synchronicity through our increased ability to celebrate our life, thereby transforming our habitual patterns into the spontaneous play of energy. The virtue of all-accomplishing action is a way of intuitively understanding that our life is meant to be lived fully, deeply, and profoundly.

## 40

# What Buddha Might Recommend

The meditations and practical applications in this chapter can help you experience the wisdom energy of wind.

### Wind Element Meditation 1

The wind element, as we've seen, is the energy of life force circulating throughout the channels of your body and throughout the networks of the phenomenal world. The cycles of breathing, the circulation of your blood, and the round of digestion, assimilation, and elimination are all expressions of the rhythmic cycle of life itself, as is the spinning of subatomic particles in their orbits, and the revolution of planets around the sun.

Begin by taking a comfortably seated position. Bring your attention to the natural cycle of your breathing. Imagine the cycle of your breathing as the medium of an unbroken circuit of energy connecting you to the world. Your breathing joins you with a vast reservoir of benevolent energy. You draw on this field of energy with each in-breath, and you also let go into it with each out-breath, feeling that you're riding on waves of energy. Unlike mindfulness practice that uses the movement of breath as a way to focus attention, in this practice the movement of breath tunes us into the vast networks of energy that sustain us and of which we are a part.

When your attention has been kidnapped by various preoccupations, simply come back to your relaxed posture and rhythmic breathing, so that there's only one thing going on—the feeling of the vital presence of energetic circulation.

### Wind Element Meditation 2

Wind is an extremely powerful erosive force. The steady force and intermittent blasts of wind can cut through granite mountains and uproot the sturdiest trees. The cutting-through quality of wind can be employed by using a labeling method. In this practice, when you experience distracting thoughts, inaudibly say "Thinking" as you cut through and dispel distracting thoughts. Immediately return your attention to the sense of presence, with your mind and body in one place. Continue to employ the labeling method to strengthen your capacity to be present.

## Practical Applications

The energy of the wind element is associated not only with our use of life force in the service of survival, but with our need to develop a sense of life direction and purpose. Our inner wind links ideas, principles, and visions into actions. Like the vast intricate networks of interconnection that sustain life on both macro and micro levels, the activity of wind radiates through every individual and throughout all of nature and culture. The following are some domains where you can practice working with the wind element.

### Bodily experience / Kinetic movement

This domain includes physical activities that promote bodily strength and endurance, balance and coordination, flexibility and muscle tone. Allow yourself about twenty minutes to take part in a simple physical activity, such as walking, stretching, yoga, free-form dancing, or a domestic activity like polishing a table, sweeping the floor, or watering plants.

The point of this practice is to sensitize yourself to the subtle energy coursing throughout your body that enables such movement. You may have to slow down in order to become aware of the actual feeling of movement and force. Pay attention to the alternation between going on automatic pilot when you perform repetitious activity, and abruptly shift to notice how each moment of activity can be fresh, rather than repetitious.

## Livelihood

Livelihood is the purposeful application of our life force or energy for both personal survival and as an expression of our compassion and creativity. The following questions will help you inquire more deeply how to connect with the energy of wind when that connection is weak.

Do you feel that your work is gratifying and meaningful—an accurate expression of who you are as a person—or just a means of earning money? How does your work help you develop specific capacities and skills, or perhaps make a social contribution? What parts of yourself does your livelihood express, and what parts does it inhibit or suppress? Can you make peace with this condition? Can you see the possibility of gradually transforming your relationship with your work so that it reflects more of who you are?

## Community and culture

Like the season of summer, wind energy could be viewed as the expression of good works through the collective. It's social consciousness longing to manifest within kinship and communal networks. Inquire whether you actively participate in your society, community, or subculture to make a contribution. Do you feel like an anonymous member of your community or society without any significant impact upon it, like a cog in a vast machine? Do you feel marginalized and disempowered because of the immensity and complexity of your society or culture? How are you establishing opportunities for belongingness and affiliation?

# Epilogue

## E Pluribus Unum

This book has been about returning to our senses so that we can discover the forgotten wisdom inherent in everyday experience. Our senses reach far beyond us, providing a bridge that connects us to other people as well as to the nonhuman world, joining us to all life on planet Earth. As we connect with the wisdom of the five elements, we're brought into direct and immediate experience of the surrounding sensory world of trees dancing in the wind, the mesmerizing rhythm of the tides, a chorus of crickets in the late afternoon, and the fragrance of freshly brewed coffee. Through the medium of our senses we experience our body and the body of the natural world as sacred and worthy of veneration.

The five elements offer a nonverbal language that inspires us to uncover the innumerable layers of ourselves and our world. They reveal the subtle energetic dimension of our experience, connecting us more deeply to the masculine and feminine polarities within ourselves and the phenomenal world. As we attune ourselves to these energies, the elements invite us into their depths, revealing what has been concealed due to our hyperindividualism, and the basic split between mind and body, between man and woman, and between us and the natural world.

Although the teachings and methods of early Buddhism show us how to deconstruct our limited notion of ego, the later left-hand teachings instruct us how to experience profound and vast identity with the wider reaches of life. This expanded sense of personhood transcends both pathological individualism and self-preserving egolessness, or what has been called the spiritual bypass.

The five wisdom energies of space, water, earth, fire, and

wind allow us to experience ourselves as inseparable from life itself. They allow us to realize that we're self-organizing systems, patterns of orderly chaos, sustained by mutual dependence and interrelationship with everything else. By working creatively with the five elements we realize that our human life is a shared life, made possible by the currents of energy that move through us, connecting us with the infinitely extended field of the cosmos. In the web of relations that sustain us, there's no absolute boundary that separates us from the rest of the world. Compassion for and care of others, human and nonhuman, is the same as care and compassion for ourselves, while we retain our distinctive and unique identity.

At our present level of evolution our species is largely preoccupied with self-protection and self-perpetuation. This preoccupation is based on a pathological notion of the self, a distorted version of individualism where we experience ourselves as separate and different not only from nonhuman life and from the natural world, but from other humans and ourselves as well.

The masculine impulse has been to separate out from Mother Nature, seeking freedom from, but ultimately control over, the natural world in the name of progress. As a collective of autonomous individual egos we've bought our tentative liberation at the price of suppressing the feminine principle within us by severing our interdependent relationship with nature, and by denying our *feeling* relationship with our own body. The current ecological crisis heralds a growing recognition of our identity with the natural world and with our own nature. There has been a groundswell of longing to reconnect with the feminine principle, to compassionately embrace the diverse community of others, both human and nonhuman.

More and more of us are experiencing the depth of our pain in response to the current ecological catastrophe and the threat of nuclear annihilation. We suffer and rejoice with our world, and we recognize our part as co-creators in the larger scheme of things. This emerging form of humanity is deeper than egolessness. It allows our heart to break open so that light can shine through to reveal that we're embedded in nature, and nature is embedded in us, and both are held by something larger. That larger something is who we are at our depth. This realization is the fruition of the left-hand path.

Our five elements are five interdependent, interpenetrating aspects of one energy—the primordial wisdom energy of life itself. The wisdom of the five elements guides us to come more directly into a feeling relationship with the community of living beings that surround and sustain human life. Our senses join us to this broader, more-than-human community and evoke genuine empathy for the current condition of devastation of our biosphere. The radically altered perception of interconnection and interdependence that the five wisdom energies provide has positive implications for how our human community can live with the tension of difference and diverse perspectives, while honoring the primacy of life itself.

Ira Rechtshaffer, summer 2018

# About the Author

Ira Rechtshaffer holds a PhD in Buddhist studies and has been a Buddhist practitioner for four decades. He practiced Zen Buddhism in Japan for four years and has been a practitioner of Tibetan or Vajrayana Buddhism since 1976. He has taught Buddhism in various seminaries, contemplative centers, and graduate programs. As a practicing psychotherapist, he integrates Buddhist and Western psychology.

He has facilitated weekly meditation groups, presenting a traditional Buddhist map for how to walk the path of everyday life with courage, dignity, and gentleness. His first book, *Mindfulness and Madness: Money, Food, Sex, and the Sacred*, can be purchased on Amazon. His website is www.wayofthemandala. Email is irarex007@att.net.

CHANGEMAKERS
BOOKS

# TRANSFORMATION

Transform your life, transform your world - Changemakers
Books publishes for individuals committed to transforming their
lives and transforming the world. Our readers seek to become
positive, powerful agents of change. Changemakers Books
inform, inspire, and provide practical wisdom and skills to
empower us to write the next chapter of humanity's future.
If you have enjoyed this book, why not tell other readers by
posting a review on your preferred book site.

# Recent bestsellers from Changemakers Books are:

### Integration
The Power of Being Co-Active in Work and Life
Ann Betz, Karen Kimsey-House
*Integration* examines how we came to be polarized in our dealing
with self and other, and what we can do to move from an either/
or state to a more effective and fulfilling way of being.
Paperback: 978-1-78279-865-1 ebook: 978-1-78279-866-8

### Bleating Hearts
The Hidden World of Animal Suffering
Mark Hawthorne
An investigation of how animals are exploited for
entertainment, apparel, research, military weapons, sport, art,
religion, food, and more.
Paperback: 978-1-78099-851-0 ebook: 978-1-78099-850-3

### Lead Yourself First!
Indispensable Lessons in Business and in Life
Michelle Ray
Are you ready to become the leader of your own life? Apply
simple, powerful strategies to take charge of yourself, your
career, your destiny.
Paperback: 978-1-78279-703-6 ebook: 978-1-78279-702-9

### Burnout to Brilliance
Strategies for Sustainable Success
Jayne Morris
Routinely running on reserves? This book helps you transform
your life from burnout to brilliance with strategies for sustainable
success.
Paperback: 978-1-78279-439-4 ebook: 978-1-78279-438-7

## Goddess Calling
Inspirational Messages & Meditations of Sacred Feminine
Liberation Thealogy
Rev. Dr. Karen Tate
A book of messages and meditations using Goddess archetypes
and mythologies, aimed at educating and inspiring those with
the desire to incorporate a feminine face of God into their
spirituality.
Paperback: 978-1-78279-442-4 ebook: 978-1-78279-441-7

## The Master Communicator's Handbook
Teresa Erickson, Tim Ward
Discover how to have the most communicative impact in this
guide by professional communicators with over 30 years of
experience advising leaders of global organizations.
Paperback: 978-1-78535-153-2 ebook: 978-1-78535-154-9

## Meditation in the Wild
Buddhism's Origin in the Heart of Nature
Charles S. Fisher Ph.D.
A history of Raw Nature as the Buddha's first teacher, inspiring
some followers to retreat there in search of truth.
Paperback: 978-1-78099-692-9 ebook: 978-1-78099-691-2

## Ripening Time
Inside Stories for Aging with Grace
Sherry Ruth Anderson
*Ripening Time* gives us an indispensable guidebook for growing
into the deep places of wisdom as we age.
Paperback: 978-1-78099-963-0 ebook: 978-1-78099-962-3

**Striking at the Roots**
A Practical Guide to Animal Activism
Mark Hawthorne
A manual for successful animal activism from an author with
first-hand experience speaking out on behalf of animals.
Paperback: 978-1-84694-091-0 ebook: 978-1-84694-653-0

Readers of ebooks can buy or view any of these bestsellers by
clicking on the live link in the title. Most titles are published
in paperback and as an ebook. Paperbacks are available in
traditional bookshops. Both print and ebook formats are available
online.

Find more titles and sign up to our readers' newsletter at
http://www.johnhuntpublishing.com/transformation
Follow us on Facebook at
https://www.facebook.com/Changemakersbooks